A LITERARY FIELD GUIDE TO SOUTHERN APPALACHIA

A Literary Field Guide to Southern Appalachia

Rose McLarney and Laura-Gray Street, EDITORS

L. L. Gaddy, NATURAL HISTORY EDITOR

The University of Georgia Press ⁓ Athens

A Wormsloe
FOUNDATION
nature book

© 2019 by the University of Georgia Press
Athens, Georgia 30602
www.ugapress.org
Designed by Erin Kirk New
Set in Arno Pro
Printed and bound by Sheridan Books
The paper in this book meets the guidelines for
permanence and durability of the Committee on
Production Guidelines for Book Longevity of the
Council on Library Resources.

Most University of Georgia Press titles are
available from popular e-book vendors.

Printed in the United States of America
23 c 5 4 3

Library of Congress Cataloging-in-Publication Data
Names: Street, Laura-Gray, editor. | Gaddy, L. L., editor. | McLarney, Rose,
    1982– editor.
Title: A literary field guide to southern Appalachia / Rose McLarney and
    Laura-Gray Street, editors ; L.L. Gaddy, natural history editor.
Description: Athens : The University of Georgia Press, [2019] | Includes
    bibliographical references.
Identifiers: LCCN 2019018159 | ISBN 9780820356242 (hardback)
Subjects: LCSH: Natural history—Appalachian Region, Southern—Poetry.
    | American poetry—21st century.
Classification: LCC PS310.N3 L58 2019 | DDC811/.60809364097569—dc23
LC record available at https://lccn.loc.gov/2019018159

Dedicated to the eastern cougar (puma, mountain lion, wildcat, catamount, painter, mountain screamer, in all its many names), in 2018 declared extinct from the region whose diversity we write to praise but must better protect.

Contents

Acknowledgments

— Thank you to Eric Magrane and Christopher Cokinos, editors of *The Sonoran Desert: A Literary Field Guide*, for the idea of a literary field guide and being willing to share it; Simmons Buntin for suggesting a literary field guide for our region; Sean Prentiss for all the help in developing our proposal; Bill McLarney for contributing the information on fish species, as well as his expertise in other aspects of the natural and human communities of the area; W. David Chamberlain, Richard White, and Jeff Lepore for their review of and comments on natural history information on various species; the Auburn University College of Liberal Arts for supporting the creation of the original artwork; the Randolph College Summer Research Program and intern and research assistant Celina Matthews (and her bearded dragon, Elsker) for help with the final stages of the manuscript; Allyson Comstock for advising us, early on, on visual art; Jay Kardan, Susan Ervin, and Justin Gardiner for editing advice and support; the Hambidge Center for the Creative Arts and Sciences; all the contributors, particularly those who revised their work or agreed to participate in the project before it was under contract; and Patrick Allen, Phyllis C. Wells, and everyone at the University of Georgia Press who has made this book possible.

A LITERARY FIELD GUIDE TO SOUTHERN APPALACHIA

Editors' Introduction

—— "Light by which I've lived, the need to name, to know," Ellen Bryant Voigt writes in "Redbud," a poem about the tree characteristic of the Virginia mountains from which she comes, as well as Linnaeus's system of classification—and about engaging with the world through both vision and language. Voigt's statement about light in "Redbud" is followed by a line about challenges: "the work of it, the cost of it." As anyone who has tried to write poetry knows, even language at its most refined may seem to fall short of that to which you want it to pay tribute. Naming, identifying, and categorizing things by scientific systems can seem reductive too, as attested by the frequency with which writing about wild lives turns to musing on their unknowability. The same is true, in different ways, for our visual renderings of the world—our illustrations, diagrams, and maps. Yet it is because we prize and want to know the natural world that as birders and botanists, writers and editors, naturalists and artists, we keep searching the fields and woods—and keep trying to depict, to articulate, what we see there.

This anthology aims to be a guide to encountering the species of Southern Appalachia not just in the scientific sense but also in the broader, artistic senses of poetry and art. Field guides originated in the 1800s, in fact, not exclusively as scientific texts with formulaic descriptions of species but as colorful books that might weave quotes from poetry or lively personal anecdotes into factual content. In our field guide, the natural history notes provide facts about the inhabitants of one of the most biodiverse ecosystems on earth but in a conversational, literary form. The poems represent another great wealth of Southern Appalachia—its rich community of writers—and combine natural history information with the work of the imagination. The illustrations, also contributed by regional creators, similarly present recognizable subjects, artistically interpreted in unique ways. We hope the diverse contents and approaches of this book honor the place—the Southern Appalachian region, an area itself variously defined and interpreted— that inspired it.

Sifting through those various definitions and interpretations of an area whose bounds are much debated, we chose to define Southern Appalachia much as John C. Campbell did in his book *The Southern Highlander and His Homeland*: "the Blue Ridge Valley, and Allegheny Ridge counties of Virginia; all of West Virginia; eastern Tennessee; eastern Kentucky; western North Carolina; the four northwestern counties of South Carolina; northern Georgia; and northeastern Alabama." We opted to be guided by Campbell because his understanding of

Appalachia was based, not on lines drawn on maps, but on cultural and natural considerations. That he did not rely on clear-cut state lines led to odd editorial discussions of, for instance, whether the hometowns of poets we admired fell on the right side of a given state or whether their past connections to the region were enough to justify inclusion in the book. As our work proceeded, these efforts at geographical precision (which is to say, enforcing already imprecise boundaries) gave way to other challenging priorities, such as adequately representing the region's biodiversity with a limited species list and collecting poems that illustrate its human diversity.

Deciding which sixty species to include from Southern Appalachia's ten thousand possibilities was a pleasant sort of difficulty. We knew our contents could not begin to be comprehensive. (After all, there are more species of fish in the state of Tennessee than in all of Europe.) But our natural history editor, L. L. Gaddy, has an unusual balance of scientific expertise and literary sensitivity, and he selected a cross-section of iconic and well-recognized species, endemic and unusual species, and endangered and threatened species. We hope that among these species intimately associated with Appalachia readers will encounter some that are engagingly familiar and some that are new and provoke curiosity about this region, where more species are discovered every year.

We hope the same is true for encounters with the poets and their poems. Some poems, such as Allison Adelle Hedge Coke's "Smallmouth Bass" or Catherine Carter's "Mountain Brook Lamprey," are dedicated entirely to their species, giving over all their words to description and praise of it. Many more poems tell something of a personal story along with speaking of the species, but this is not to say they co-opt the poem with the insertion of an "I." Lesley Wheeler writes about a woman's troubles, but she does so with words that speak equally to the black walnut: "Tell me your tough- / shelled fruit and I will tell you / mine." Michael McFee, writing of the happiness he has had in "Please," can only hope to have his ashes consumed by what he acknowledges is the far greater glory of the rhododendron in the end. Some poets align their subject species with examinations of larger human history and culture, as Sean Hill does in "Lake Sturgeon," which is also about the legacy of the Civil War, and as Rebecca Gayle Howell does in "On the Appalachian Wild Turkey (Or, a Little Capitalist Ditty Hillbillies Learn the Hour We Are Born)," with a title and subtitle that demonstrate the poem's dual purposes. The view of other poems pans wider still, as in Adrian Blevins's "Fox Heart." This sweeping poem includes whole ecosystems, a long list of other species names, brand names of chain stores, and personal stories about connections to the land, while keeping the fox at its heart. "Long Mountain Otter" by Elizabeth Seydel Morgan is about an otter—an otter as interpreted by a poet's language and, what's more, as represented by an artist, carving rock. Morgan is writing about a sculpture. Yet, layers removed as the original animal may be, she is still contemplating the real otter; the value of the poetic homage is real. Morgan tells us, "Born wet out of stone, / it doesn't matter what he's not. / The Long Mountain Otter is freed to be." The poems in this book should be a kind of freeing too, because when subjectivity takes the form of admiration, it can be a positive force.

Representing the region's poetic diversity was also an important aspiration for us. If we could not achieve it fully, we do hope readers find their intellectual landscapes enlarged by the sampling provided here. We are happy that more than half of the book's contributors are women, and that there is a spectrum of styles, as seen in the forms ranging from L. Lamar Wilson's sonnet "Whip-poor-will, I" to contemporary inventions such as Glenis Redmond's golden shovel for ginseng, "Living Jazz," and from Anna Lena Phillips Bell's drivel-generator-composed "Flowere and Are: A Charm for Chestnut" to Kevin McIlvoy's prose poem for the mollycrawbottom, "Thank You For." McIlvoy's poem describes the fish's movement with a highway metaphor: "the speeding traffic of hatchery rainbows muscles untamed old Appalachian browns to exit lanes and into streams and under crumbling cutbanks on poison-crusted agricorporate land." This place-based writing isn't all idyllic, and the Appalachia of these poems isn't all hollers (though Melissa Range's "Tulip Poplar" does offer one, in a poem with a "hell-no," back-talking strength too great to be mistaken as trite). There are Rita Mae Reese's deer mice in labs ("The Natural History of Model Organisms") and Lisa Lewis's Fraser firs in tree farms ("HUSBANDRY   COMMERCE   SENTIMENT") too. That said, there are of course plenty of poems that seek solace and retreat, such as John Lane's "Crotalus Horridus," in which he takes the reader into the forest in pursuit of "relief / from being too human."

Most of the poems in *A Literary Field Guide to Southern Appalachia* were written specifically for this project; however, we have also included a few previously published poems by notable American poets connected to the region, such as Wendell Berry, Ellen Bryant Voigt, Robert Morgan, and Mary Oliver (who spent significant time in the environment surrounding Sweet Briar College in Virginia). By intention, the poets in the anthology are contemporary and, with a few exceptions, living. We couldn't *not* include work by the late and great Irene McKinney, former poet laureate of West Virginia. Mary Oliver, who wrote some of the most beloved contemporary American nature poems, was alive when we undertook this project. She passed away during the editing process, but her place in the book remains clear, as does her influence on so many writers. And, sadly, Kathryn Stripling Byer also passed away after writing her poem "To *Pterophylla Camellifolia* at the Winter Solstice" for the katydid but before this anthology was completed. We cannot sufficiently express our gratitude for the opportunity to correspond with Byer about the relief she found in focusing on this vigorous poem, which is about looking forward to emerging into spring and the unfurling lifelines running through creatures, while undergoing chemotherapy, and for the opportunity to keep her words alive in this book.

We are grateful to all the poets of Southern Appalachia, those with work on these pages and others we don't yet know about or couldn't include. Thank you to the abundant talent and ongoing literary legacy of the region. The process of editing *A Literary Field Guide to Southern Appalachia* has made us believe even more adamantly than when we began in the richness of our place and its writing. We also had the opportunity to work with seven artists who have contributed their own signature touches to images of Southern Appalachia's species. We are grateful for the elegant delineations of Allyson Comstock's work, with a detail characteristic of each species repeating in that image's top and bottom borders; the sumptuous precision of Billy Renkl's constructed designs; the immersive calligraphic iconography of Suzanne Stryk's pieces; Landon Godfrey's muscular, energetic imagery; Gary Hawkins's structural wit in his layered compositions; Dan Powell's delicate and meditative watercolor drawings; and Henry Shearon's renderings, which convey both tranquil absorption and alert intelligence. We have to acknowledge at this point in the introduction that we, as poets, have focused largely on the written aspects of the anthology and left ourselves with fewer words to spare for our artists, but we also know that these images, which have inspired us in the process of putting the book together and, in some cases, galvanized the poets as they were refining their poems, are powerful and articulate enough to speak for themselves.

Christoph Irmscher wrote in the introduction to *The Poetics of Natural History* of "the naturalist who creates a collection and then puts himself into it," representing his own tastes as much as his supposed subject. These words could also describe the editorial process—attempting to make an inclusive collection but, of course, making decisions based on our own ways of thinking—and the creative writing process, in which the poet must shape the content. Painter, ornithologist, and naturalist John James Audubon lamented that he couldn't adequately describe the wood thrush. In James Davis May's poem about that same bird for this book, May laments, "So much absence in art: the bird we can't see, / the song we can't describe." As editors (and poets and humans), we know our perceptions, our categories, and sometimes our choices are imperfect. We hear the truth in Gyorgyi Voros's "Single-Sorus Spleenwort (*Asplenium monanthes*)," scoffing that words such as "rare, endangered, prized" that people apply don't matter to plants. At the same time, a poet's choice of words *can* make all the difference for a human reader, and we are proud to present the sixty poems we are able to publish here.

This literary field guide aims to cultivate a different kind of apprehension than the field guides considered standard today. (There are better books to refer to if you want to-the-point tools for exact identification.) We like to imagine readers using this anthology in the field: carrying it outdoors to sit and read, taking it in hand while they walk and look. But even if you read this in a fluorescent-lit classroom or a plane's pressurized cabin and recirculated air, by reading as carefully as poetry requires, you will practice receptivity to what is outside yourself, which is also a form of field study. We hope you read conventional field guides as well. And read *The Sonoran Desert: A Literary Field Guide*, whose editors, Eric Magrane and Christopher Cokinos, launched this multidisciplinary concept; we are indebted to them. Let us expand the attentiveness to the cultural and natural beauties these books prompt into a caring that values every place and each life form and believes they deserve to be preserved.

Holly Haworth writes about the chucky madtom in "Through the Burning World You Blazed":

> You double-helixed stroke of luck,
> I am losing the use for your name
> soon after I've named you,
> you cryptic flicker of language.
> My tongue plies the silence of eons
> like your dorsal did the bedrock waters.
>
> And when did the tense of you shift?
> (Or has it yet?— foolish hope I hold onto.)

The regret in these lines intimates that loss is an inevitability. Yet to discover this ambitious poem (coming from one of the anthology's younger contributors) feels like another forward-looking stroke of luck. And the poem is joyful in that it wants nothing more than the already given wonders of this world. In his poem on the persimmon, Maurice Manning conveys the grace of those moments when your mind becomes a place nature is allowed to occupy. It is with his words from "And Too Much Beauty in the Sky" that we will leave you—which is to say, send you forward into the rest of the book:

I wish the world were a better place
sometimes, but I won't wish it now,
there's too much fluttering and grace,
and too much beauty in the sky—
there's too much beauty in the sky
to wish the world were otherwise.

Rose McLarney
Laura-Gray Street

— The Appalachian Mountains extend from northern Alabama and Georgia and northwestern South Carolina north to Newfoundland. The name was probably derived from that of an early Native American tribe or Native American place-name in southeastern North America. In early colonial America, most of what we now think of as the Appalachians was called the Alleghenies. In the early 1800s, it was even proposed that the United States be named Appalachia or Alleghania. Today, the terms "Allegheny" or "Alleghany" usually refer to portions of the middle Appalachians in the Ohio River drainage system, such as the Allegheny Plateau. In the north, the common pronunciation of "Appalachians" is "Appalayshuns"; to the south, the same mountain range is generally referred to as the "Appalatchuns." Both pronunciations are considered correct.

This literary field guide covers the Southern Appalachians, a region defined as those portions of the Blue Ridge, Valley and Ridge, and Appalachian Plateau physiographic provinces of West Virginia, Kentucky, Virginia, Tennessee, Alabama, Georgia, North Carolina, and South Carolina. Included in this large area (among many other less-well-known but interesting areas) are several noteworthy mountain subregions: the Allegheny Plateau in West Virginia and Cumberland Plateau in Kentucky, Tennessee, and Alabama; Sand Mountain in Alabama; Lookout Mountain in Tennessee and Georgia; the Blue Ridge Escarpment gorges of North Carolina, South Carolina, and Georgia; the Little Tennessee River basin; the Great Smoky Mountains in Tennessee and North Carolina; the Black Mountains in North Carolina; Roan Mountain massif in North Carolina and Tennessee; Mount Rogers massif in Virginia; and the New River basin in North Carolina, Virginia, and West Virginia.

GEOLOGIC HISTORY

The Appalachians are an ancient mountain range. Rocks in the Roan Mountain massif on the Tennessee–North Carolina border are estimated to be 1.8 billion years old, among the oldest ever dated. The proto–Appalachian Mountains date as far back as the Caledonian orogeny, a mountain building period of 480 to 390 million years ago, when mountain range extending from Scandinavia through what is now Scotland into New England and southward (possibly as far as Alabama) was uplifted. Europe was part of North America on the supercontinent Pangaea at that time; after the breakup of Pangaea, about 350 to 260 million years ago, during what is called the Appalachian or Alleghanian orogeny, Africa collided with eastern North America (possibly several times), forming a mountain range with peaks as high as the present-day Alps or Rockies. After millions of years of erosion, the Appalachians were only about as high as our present-day Piedmont. A final uplift, however, took place in the Mesozoic Period (about seventy million years ago), creating a higher mountain mass. Since this most recent uplift, the downcutting of streams and rivers has formed the moderately elevated, dissected, tree-covered mountain range that we now know as the Appalachians.

Geologically, the Southern Appalachian Mountains are dominated by three major physiographic provinces—the Blue Ridge, the Valley and Ridge, and the Appalachian Plateau. The Blue Ridge (sometimes called the Blue Ridge Thrust Belt) is a mass of crust thrust "over" the old Valley and Ridge. Here, crystalline (igneous and metamorphic) rocks dominate. The Blue Ridge crest reaches up to six thousand feet or higher (Grandfather Mountain). The Valley and Ridge is an old sedimentary basin with complex folds, forming ridges and valleys. The rocks here are limestone, shales, chert, and other sedimentary types. Elevations in the Valley and Ridge generally do not exceed three thousand feet. The Appalachian Plateau is made up of the Cumberland Plateau and the Allegheny Plateau, both west of the Blue Ridge and the Valley and Ridge. Here, sedimentary rock has been uplifted and has metamorphosed into harder rock such as schists and slates. The Allegheny Plateau rises more than five thousand feet in height in West Virginia.

HUMAN HISTORY

Humans arrived in the Southern Appalachians more than twelve thousand years ago. In what is called the Archaic Period, various types (tribes) of Native Americans lived in the Southern Appalachians, probably as hunter-gatherers. By the time Europeans began to communicate with the natives, only the Cherokees were present in the Southern Appalachians. These Native Americans subsisted on a complex mixture of farming and hunting and gathering wild animals and plants. Describing Keowee Valley (a lower Cherokee settlement) in the late 1700s, William Bartram said: "These vales and swelling bases of surrounding hills, afford vast crops of excellent grass and herbage fit for pasturage and hay; of the latter Plantago Virginica, Sanguisorba, Geum, Fragaria [strawberry] &c. The Panax quinquefolium or Ginseng, now appears plentiful on the North exposure of the hill, growing out of rich, mellow humid earth."

Spanish explorers (Hernando de Soto and Juan Pardo) traversed the Southern Appalachians in the early 1500s but established no settlements or trade. The mountains were considered the western frontier of North America until the early

1700s. Trading posts were created near major Cherokee towns during this period. Settlements were eventually constructed near the trading posts after settlers made peace with the Cherokees (though several Cherokee towns were razed during the "peace"-making process). To travel there from coastal North America, one needed horses, a guide, and time to spare. The Southern Appalachians were the outback in those times. Because of the remoteness of the interior and the difficulty of traveling there, distances were exaggerated. Mark Catesby, a naturalist who explored Carolina in the early 1700s, said of some Blue Ridge plants: "They grow on the Banks of the Savanna River, about five hundred Miles from the Mouth of it." In fact, the Blue Ridge is fewer than three hundred miles from Savannah.

In the 1800s the Southern Appalachians were rapidly being settled by English, Welsh, Germans, and Scots from the Piedmont and Coastal Plains (Gulf and Atlantic) and Germans and Scotch-Irish from the north (Pennsylvania northward). The Scotch-Irish settlers probably outnumbered all, drawn to the possibilities of small-scale and pastoral life, reminiscent of their origins in Scotland and Northern Ireland. In the mid-1800s large cities began to prosper in the Southern Appalachians. Among them were Huntington, West Virginia; the Valley and Ridge cities of Virginia (Harrisonburg, Roanoke, and Blacksburg) and Tennessee (Knoxville); Charlottesville and Lynchburg, Virginia, on the Blue Ridge front; Boone and Asheville in the Blue Ridge of North Carolina; Chattanooga on the Tennessee River; and in Alabama, Huntsville on the Highland Rim of the Cumberlands and Birmingham near the southern end of the Valley and Ridge.

BIODIVERSITY AND SPECIES RICHNESS

The Southern Appalachians consitute one of the richest regions in North America in total species. Because of the range of elevations in the region (from 1,000 to 6,600 feet), enormous habitat variation exists. Spruce-fir forests cover the peaks of the Black Mountains, the Roan Mountain massif, the Smokies, and peaks as far south as the Balsams (near Waynesville, North Carolina, at the thirty-fifth parallel north). The rocky high elevations harbor alpine species such as the wine-leaved cinquefoil—known as far north as Greenland and as far south as northern Georgia. Northern hardwood forests common in the Adirondacks and New England flourish in the Southern Appalachians at 3,000 to 5,000 feet, and in nutrient-rich ravines and coves and gulfs on the Cumberland Plateau, home to a species-rich hardwood forest type with a spectacular array of showy wildflower species.

Great Smoky Mountains National Park alone hosts around 125 species of trees. (For comparison, the entire Pacific Northwest has around 90 species of trees.) The gorges of the southern Blue Ridge are rich in mosses—Whitewater River Gorge, with over 250 species, has more types of mosses than any other site in North America. Finally, the species diversity of salamanders, millipedes, and fungi in the Southern Appalachians far exceeds that in other regions of North America.

Scientists have described approximately ten thousand species of organisms, five thousand of which are vascular plants, from this rich and diverse region (and many species remain undescribed). From all of these, we have selected sixty noteworthy species for our guide. Our selection process was somewhat arbitrary, but we tried to include common, rare, and otherwise interesting species from a wide range of taxonomic groups. In the end, we have no doubt omitted an important or favorite species here or there, but we think these species should allow for an interesting literary and artistic journey through the Southern Appalachians.

MAJOR HABITATS AND PLANT COMMUNITIES

We have selected species from each of the ten major habitats found in the Southern Appalachians. In the following discussions, asterisks mark species our field guide highlights. All taxonomic nomenclature used in this book is from www.itis.gov, with the exception of *Amanita jacksonii*, which is covered in www.catalogueoflife.org.

Spruce-Fir Forests

Spruce-fir forests are dominated by red spruce and Fraser fir* and occur at the highest elevations of the Southern Appalachians—from approximately 4,000 to 6,600 feet. Both of these evergreen species create dark forests with mossy understories. Mountain paper birch, yellow birch, and other northern species also occur in the canopy of this type. Notable spruce-fir areas are Roan Mountain, the Black Mountains, the Smokies, and the southern Blue Ridge Parkway.

Grassy and Shrub Balds

Grassy and shrub balds are high-elevation nonforested plant communities dominated by grasses or shrubs such as great laurel, Catawba rhododendron,* and mountain laurel. Balds were originally thought to be natural environments, but research has shown that they may be anthropogenic in nature (caused by logging, fire, or grazing, for example). Some of the shrub balds in the Southern Appalachians, such as Craggy Gardens, north of Asheville, or Roan Mountain, on the North Carolina–Tennessee line at near six thousand feet, have spectacular shrub blooms in late spring and early summer.

High-Elevation Rocky Knobs and Domes

High-elevation rocky knobs and domes, such as Blowing Rock and Devil's Courthouse in North Carolina, are nonforested high-elevation habitats with little or no vegetation. These habitats are highly stressed by wind and cold winter temperatures and are dominated by northern dwarfed shrub, herbaceous, and graminaceous species such as the wine-leaved cinquefoil.*

Northern Hardwood Forests

Northern hardwood forests are found between three thousand and five thousand feet elevation and include trees such as beech, sugar maple, red oak, yellow birch, and yellow buckeye. They have more in common with New England forests than with most southern forests. Northern hardwood forests are common on the northwest slopes of Mount Rogers in Virginia and on Sugar Mountain in the Boone, North Carolina, area. The American black bear* and the ruffed grouse are common in this habitat.

Pine-Oak and Heath Forests

Pine-oak and heath forests are widespread in the Southern Appalachians. They occur at lower to mid-elevations on dry ridges and slopes. Generally dominated by white pine, pitch pine, and shortleaf pine, they also include white oak, scarlet oak, and chestnut oak in the canopy. Their understories are dominated by thickets of heaths such as mountain laurel, great laurel, and various species of blueberries. Numerous generalist species (species that live in various conditions) discussed in the text are found in this plant community.

Cove Forests

Cove forests are found at mid- to low elevations in nutrient-rich ravines and colluvial coves and gulfs (a term used for incised coves in the Cumberland Plateau). Often rich in calcium, magnesium, and other bases, the cove forest is usually found on cool north-facing slopes. The forest flora of such coves have been referred to as the "mixed mesophytic forest," a forest rich in tree and herbaceous species. Dominant trees in the Southern Appalachian cove forest include sugar maple, tulip poplar,* white ash, basswood, white walnut (butternut), black walnut,* and silverbell. In the richest coves, the canopy trees reach more than one hundred feet in height with trunks more than three feet in diameter.

In addition to their arboreal richness, such forests harbor a ground layer rich in spring-flowering herbaceous species. Often called wildflower coves, such coves host a diverse flora of spring ephemerals and showy herbaceous species such as trout lily, bloodroot,* spring beauty, violets, orchids, and other spring-flowering plants. In these coves, thousands of flowering plants are frequently present in April and May. Wildflower lovers flock to such areas, many of which are locally famous.

The Smokies and the Cumberland Plateau gulfs have some of the richest cove forests in the region. But most areas in the Southern Appalachians have their own local wildflower coves: Newsome Sinks in northern Alabama, the Pocket and Cloudland Canyon in northwestern Georgia, Tamassee Falls (also known as Lee Falls) and Station Cove in northwestern South Carolina, Hickory Nut Gorge and Chimney Rock in North Carolina and the innumerable high-elevation coves on the southern Blue Ridge Parkway in North Carolina.

Cove forests are quite variable in species presence and dominance throughout the range of this book. Some such forests are dominated by tulip poplar,* others by sugar maple; some have scattered stands of Canadian hemlock* within coves or ravines. Species such as bloodroot,* ginseng,* black walnut,* and tulip poplar* are all found in rich cove forests.

Gorges

Gorges are scattered throughout the Southern Appalachians where rivers have cut deeply into the local rock. The southern Blue Ridge Escarpment gorges of North Carolina, South Carolina, and Georgia harbor rare tropical ferns unknown elsewhere in North America. The French Broad River and the New River have cut deep gorges in North Carolina, Virginia, and West Virginia. Carolina gorge moss* and single-sorus spleenwort* grow in escarpment gorges in North Carolina, South Carolina, and Georgia, and the persistent trillium* is endemic to one small gorge in South Carolina and in Tallulah Gorge in Georgia.

Alluvial and Riparian Forests

Alluvial and riparian forests are bottomland and streamside forests of low to mid-elevations. These are the floodplain forests of the French Broad, the Little Tennessee, the New River, the Chattooga, and other Appalachian rivers and streams. River birch, sycamore, green ash, black walnut,* and black willow are common canopy trees in this habitat type.

Other Wetland Communities

Water communities include bogs, fens, lakes, beaver ponds, swamps, rivers, streams, and aquatic habitats. Bogs are typically nonforested wetlands with acidic soils, while fens, rarer in the Southern Appalachians, are nonforested wetlands with calcium-rich soils. A good fen is found on Bluff Mountain in North Carolina, and excellent examples of Southern Appalachian bogs are found in the Pink Beds in North Carolina and the Cranberry Glades and Dolly Sods in West Virginia. While natural lakes are also rare in the Southern Appalachians—most lakes in the region are constructed—beaver ponds are common along low-gradient streams and occur up to four thousand feet. Many wetland habitats formerly present in the region have been filled in for development or drained for agriculture. Aquatic habitats here include surface and underwater realms of rivers, streams, ponds, and lakes where fish, insect larvae and pupae, and tadpoles live. These habitats also support otters,* beavers,* great blue herons,* bullfrogs,* painted turtles,* spring peepers,* and many other species.

Meadows and Old Fields

Meadows and old fields are human-made environments, but they are rich in species and important in the biodiversity of the Southern Appalachians. In spring, mountain meadows are filled with the beauty and richness of native and introduced grasses and wildflowers. In autumn, Joe Pye weed, ironweed,* goldenrods, and asters dominate meadows. Old abandoned fields illustrate the natural succession from field to forest. At low elevations old fields are gradually seeded with pine species, while at middle to higher elevation and in moist coves, tulip poplar* invades.

L. L. Gaddy

I ～ Trees and Plants

HABITAT AND RANGE: Low ridges, midslopes, lower slopes, and coves.

DESCRIPTION AND NOTES: When European settlers arrived, about one in every four trees in the Appalachians was a chestnut. Up to one hundred feet in height, the giant chestnut was valued for its rot-resistant wood and its "carroty-tasting" nut, a major food source for animals ranging from livestock to the eastern black bear. In 1904 a pathogenic fungus that became known as the chestnut blight was introduced to New York City from Japan via nursery stock. By the 1940s chestnuts throughout the East had succumbed and died, a decimation on the scale of that of the passenger pigeon or bison. The loss of this resource—the income from timber and the beauty of the trees—was particularly acute in the rural economy of the Southern Appalachians. But the saplings that still sprout tenaciously, if briefly, from diseased stumps have spurred tireless work to engineer blight-resistant strains and resurrect the chestnut's ancient grandeur.

— *Anna Lena Phillips Bell*

Flowere and Are
A charm for chestnut

Flowerer, burrer, who grew and still grow,
springing from centuries' roots each year—
thin stems, stubborn and glad, a green law
of toothed leaves lifted to flutter and flare
and yellow and fall over sloped forest floor.
Saplinget, sprouthern benearly, resistical,
toughestnut, risinget aftern devaster,
sun-seekinget standant—repear, foresist.

Flocks of cream catkins, limbs done up in snow,
bud, flood, and floor us—scent midsummer air,
funk loosened and drifting down canopy, hollow,
telling the bees your nectar is here.
Hem hillsidely slopen, persisticky ofter,
abunderal sprountain abovering, mistical,
bloominget covery, flowere and are—
sun-seekinget standant, repear, foresist.

Set seed. Send prickly burrs bursting from boughs
for chipmunk and turkey, squirrel and bear,
to save over winter or savor right now.
Abundred wholes bestnut, existand, nappear—
burstory, nestnut—neath mistance, benear.
Pinest, othemlocks, towardwood persistical,
seedlingent reachinget, vering, emer,
sun-seekinget standant, repear, foresist. ✓

Commonarchy, come and be crowned again, wear
leaf upon leaf, know sap flow and signal.
Mountainough, appinest, saplingly ver,
sun-seekinget standant—repear, foresist. ✓

great diction – very scientific sounding but works well

alliteration! all. over.

refrain

sorta rhyme?

Note: This poem's sources include research on the history of chestnut blight and text imagining favorable conditions for the chestnut. The combined source text was fed into an n-gram generator set at order 3, created by Brian Hayes.

American Ginseng   *Panax quinquefolius*

HABITAT AND RANGE: Rich woods and cove hardwood forests, usually with showy wildflowers in deciduous forests.

DESCRIPTION AND NOTES: American ginseng or "sang" is a long-lived perennial herb in the ivy family. Knee-high with palmately compound toothed leaves, it is sought after for its valuable root. American ginseng was so valuable in the eighteenth century, replacing rare Chinese ginseng as a choice aid to healing, digestion, and virility, that Daniel Boone himself gathered and sold it because it was more lucrative than the hunting and trapping he was renowned for. This rhizome—which takes years to mature and often resembles a tiny wizened and grizzled man—flowers in spring and is treasured harvest when it fruits bright red berries in the fall. Formerly common in fertile coves, ginseng is now rare due to overcollection, though Appalachian folk still gather the root for personal use and enjoyment. As one elderly woman from eastern Tennessee said, according to Anthony Cavender in *Folk Medicine in Southern Appalachia*, "When I feel down in the dumps, I go sangin."

— *Glenis Redmond*

Living Jazz

> When you have fever she wrap you up in cabbage leaves or ginseng leaves.
> —Mary Ella Grandberry, enslaved woman from Richmond, Virginia

Our lips sing your red berry praise, 'cause we
rooted in your flower flag offering for real.

Under soil, sun and shade cool
"Follow the old ways," grandma says. We

walk her path. Carry what's left
of wisdom from the oldest school.

"The scarred ones are best." So we
chew the bitter root while others lurk

Ginseng.

(*Panax quinquefolium. Linn.*)

under the cover of green shade into the late
we know how they hunt. We

hear tools clash and strike,
but we know your medicine cuts fever straight,

quells the heart and quiets what ails. Loudest we
hear the Cherokee sing,

the land is sacred and bears no sin.
Let the root bring forth lust. For we

know what our elders warn is never thin.
Troubled mouths prefer to toss back gin.

No doctor's care for us, so with poultices we
mishmash and make-do living jazz.

Ginseng, you sing loudest and proudest in June.
Hear us sing too. Read *sang*. We

dance and shout your glory, but never shout die
for death hunts us *soon and very soon.*

Stanza / interesting enjambment
but one its effective

American Persimmon

Diospyros virginiana

HABITAT AND RANGE: Deciduous forests and forest margins. Found throughout eastern North America from Connecticut south to Florida and west to Kansas.

DESCRIPTION AND NOTES: Persimmon is a dioecious tree, which means male and female reproductive parts appear on separate plants. Usually, it is the fruit-bearing female that draws notice—a small tree along a hedgerow bearing unripe persimmons that hang rose-purple against the autumn sky. It is also a tree of rich woods, where it reaches nearly one hundred feet in height. A member of the same family as ebony, its hard wood was used to make veneer and custom golf drivers. Yet the tree is most famous for its fruit. You will remember your first bite of persimmon unpleasantly if you do not know to select one that has started to darken and shrivel—signs it is ready to eat, not that it is rotting. The tannins in an immature persimmon fill the mouth with a bitter flavor and a dry feeling. As the fruit turns less attractive in appearance, and after first frost (according to folk wisdom), the soft orange inside becomes sweet. The taste is so sweet, the fruit is also known as sugarplum. Other names are simmon and possumwood—and how pleased wildlife, and even domesticated animals, including some dogs, are to find a persimmon.

— *Maurice Manning*

And Too Much Beauty in the Sky

Some thirty feet above at the roof
of the spindly persimmon tree the fruits
appear in celestial calm to adorn
this portion of the chapel ceiling.
I like this kind of architecture—
there are cedar columns and several trees
are bent to arches suspending nothing.
There is no symmetry—I'll say it
again, there is no symmetry,
because the form is designed to move
in all dimensions at once when called.
It must accommodate the wind,
but then the wind inspires the form
and birds fly freely through to utter
their joy or anguish. But I don't feel
the sting of anguish here. You'd think

with all this structure everything
would be solemn and poised to be explained.
Yet I am moving through the form,
and can't explain myself or why
it doesn't matter that I can't.
Am I a form inside another
patient, listing, silent form?
Not everything requires a reason—
I've said good-bye to certain reasons.
I wish the world were a better place
sometimes, but I won't wish it now,
there's too much fluttering and grace,
and too much beauty in the sky—
there's too much beauty in the sky
to wish the world were otherwise.

metaphor and/
or reference
to faith/
church?

TREES AND PLANTS

Black Walnut

Juglans nigra

HABITAT AND RANGE: Rich bottomlands, riparian areas, and cove forests.

DESCRIPTION AND NOTES: The black walnut's deeply furrowed bark etches the tree with its distinctive pitch-dark cast. This towering native of the Southern Appalachians grows in lush bottomlands and on stream banks with other rich-soil-loving species, such as white ash and pawpaw, and sometimes in wildflower coves. It is also found around old home places and farmsteads, where it was planted for shade and other uses. This slow-growing species, once abundant, is now overharvested and diminishing. The dark, fine-grained heartwood, so prized for furniture, gunstocks, and veneer, attracts "walnut rustlers," such as a Kentucky man who was sentenced and fined in 2016 for illegally harvesting a black walnut stand. Meanwhile, the roots carry on their own black-market operations, exuding a natural herbicide—juglone—that kills or stunts certain plants within growing range. The compound leaves have an astringent odor. The corrugated nut, though irksome to collect and crack, is worth the time and effort. (Homemade black walnut ice cream is an unparalleled gourmet treat.) Juice from green hulls is a folk remedy for ringworm, and the pulverized shells are used to drill oil wells and clean jet engines. Walnuts provide food for woodpeckers, deer, foxes, and squirrels and are the preferred host of luna and regal moths.

— *Lesley Wheeler*

Black Walnut Tree

How do you persist, knowing
your shadow is poisonous?
How do you bear the thirst
driving your taproot through
5 silty clay, toward creek or sewer,
seeking more and more water?
The same power helping you
grow strong and straight,
heartwood densely grained,
10 leaflets velvet, serrate—
it pushes others away.
You deep-grooved volunteer,
magnificent citizen sickening
my yard: I need to learn

metaphor for the self in
relation to loved ones / others?

enjambment here. can read as
individual ideas of self n
tree.

how to endure my own
bitterness. Tell me your tough-
shelled fruit and I will tell you
mine, as I render the ground
unkind. Chemistry of hunger,
ambition. Bound to harm,
whether or not we rue it.

TREES AND PLANTS

Bloodroot   *Sanguinaria canadensis*

HABITAT AND RANGE: Rich, moist deciduous forests.

DESCRIPTION AND NOTES: To walk Southern Appalachian woods in early March and find the first bloodroot flower—broad, pristine white petals arrayed around yolk-yellow stamens—is to know spring has begun. These ephemeral flowers disappear within days, however, and seedpods form: long capsules with pursed tips where seeds ripen. The seeds have large elaiosomes or oil-bodies that provide food for ants, which in turn disperse the seeds of the plant, a symbiotic process called myrmecochory. Although bloodroot has a long history as a medicinal plant, many of its uses have been proven more toxic and caustic than curative, although sanguinarine, a bloodroot extract, has been approved by the U.S. Food and Drug Administration as an antiplaque and antibacterial agent for toothpastes and mouthwashes. And dye is still made from the blood-red sap that, oozing from cut roots, gave the sanguine plant its name.

— *Sandra Meek*

Still Life with Bloodroot

Brain-veined, cabbaged
around a single bud, in barest canopy
your one-winged leaf unfurls
to a lemon crown of anthers, to ghostwhite petals' quick
thinning to translucence, to capsule
unzipping its pod of pursed seeds nut-brown, glossy
as tiger eye, elaiosomes' umbilical froth
coiling each globed bead—the dormant future figured
as apple, and worm, though your whole
is generative: even these filmy members
winnow ants—copper baubles spider-wired
to filigree—feed their young, leaving the seed to sprout
from nest debris. There are those who thrive
in margins, who survive the wild
shrinking: coyote, raccoon, dandelion, fire ants
overrunning forest and field, who take the bait but
destroy the seed. Outsiders, can we help
but hunger? Bloodroot, you unscroll
to the staggered world of fence posts

[handwritten margin note: accurate description of animals]

no new flowers. Your given name a study in slicing
a clotted root to bleed, this world so beautiful
we could eat you whole: Blood Root,
Red Root, Tetterwort, Sweet Slumber—nest
I call you by, scouting your woods;
whether as winnow—or fire—I come
to you, what begins each spring
one more vanishing.

Canada Hemlock

Tsuga canadensis

HABITAT AND RANGE: Found mostly in cool coves but sometimes also on rock outcrops, especially on north-facing slopes. Along the Appalachian Mountains to Georgia and northern Alabama.

DESCRIPTION AND NOTES: These small-coned conifers are remarkably slow growing and long lived, maturing at three hundred years and living for maybe eight hundred (the oldest recorded hemlock was just shy of a thousand years). This species, also called eastern hemlock, has feathery foliage softer in form and texture than that of other conifers. The high tannin content of its bark made it valuable in the late nineteenth and early twentieth centuries for tanning leather, brown dyes, and medicinal salves. As a foundation species, eastern hemlock creates its unique ecosystem. But today that dynamic is threatened by the hemlock woolly adelgid, a sap-sucking invasive that was first discovered in Virginia in 1951 and swathes the conifer's shimmering needles with masses of white, wooly eggs. A 2009 study found that the wooly adelgid was spreading faster than expected in the Southern Appalachians, the same area devastated by the chestnut blight in the early 1900s.

— *Laura Long*

The Singing Hemlock
(*Tsuga canadensis*)

My mother remembers two tall hemlocks
on either side of the farmhouse porch in 1935—
she sat there as a child and listened to them singing
all up and down their bodies,
their whirling, plunging, twirl-fanned branches.

For eleven years I lived next to a tall old hemlock.
A hemlock is the dark when the night is green,
a storm nudging a lake into shaggy fans,
a dancer when the cape is tasseled
with beads of cone-buds,

patience when the path to unfiltered sunlight
takes centuries. Hardwood trees fall away
and the hemlock rises from a spare sapling,
more space than branches,
to a pagoda 800 years old

or more—no one knows for sure.
A three-inch tree may be 200 years old,
a ten-inch 350. Though beetles
have felled many old hemlocks now
new ones will rise and the deer

will bed beneath them, legs folded
like ladders put away for the moment,
the does and young nestled together,
sheltered from the snow, hearing a song
as old and new as the moon rise.

imagery / enjambment

Carolina Gorge Moss   *Plagiomnium carolinianum*

HABITAT AND RANGE: Often under the spray of waterfalls or other moist, shaded rock cliffs in North Carolina, South Carolina, Georgia, and Tennessee. This moss is found in fewer than ten localities in these four states.

DESCRIPTION AND NOTES: The gorges and ravines of the Southern Appalachians are rich with mosses, harboring more than a third of the moss species of North America. Three hundred species have been identified in Whitewater Gorge along the North Carolina–South Carolina state line in the Blue Ridge escarpment region. That means those three miles contain nearly three-fourths as many mosses as are in all of California. It was in this gorge, behind the sheet of water from Whitewater Falls, that the late Lewis Anderson of Duke University came across Carolina gorge moss—a new species, which he described in 1954. Since then additional populations of the still-rare Carolina gorge moss have been found by botanists and naturalists in the gorge region of the Southern Appalachians. Most of these locations are now protected from disturbance. Carolina gorge moss is so rare that there are no previously extant photographic images or scientific drawings of the species. Note the distinctive details of this small plant (dark green in nature), which the artist has rendered based on descriptions. The leaves are five to eight millimeters in length—long for a moss.

— *Justin Gardiner*

On the Way to Three Forks Pool

I've walked for miles through this current—
slow rush over lichened rock,
over numbed feet, over the deep

green shade of shallow pools
coursing far back into spruce woods.
This isn't about a finding.

Not a startled bear bounding up the hillside,
or a species of moss so rare
that even if it was here, I wouldn't know

what to look for. It is enough,
simply, to trust that no one will
chance upon me here, that I won't speak

a word aloud for days. I have known
such trailless places before,
though they were all on the other side

of this riven country—the redolent
duff of Pacific old growth,
and rivers swollen fast by snowmelt.

A stone can become so polished
by a stream's steady pull that it lifts off
and becomes that stream. A person

can live so long away from home
that another place stands in for home,
for a time at least. I'm learning now

to be at rest, like some quiet being
obscured by laurel thickets,
by a gorge's carved cutbanks.

Like a moss that burrows in
behind a waterfall's thrall and push.
Not documented or drawn

by anyone—left off, like this place,
from all the known maps. Stay
hidden from us. Remind us

of the merits of damp thickening dark.
Prompt us toward those places
with no route to them we could have seen.

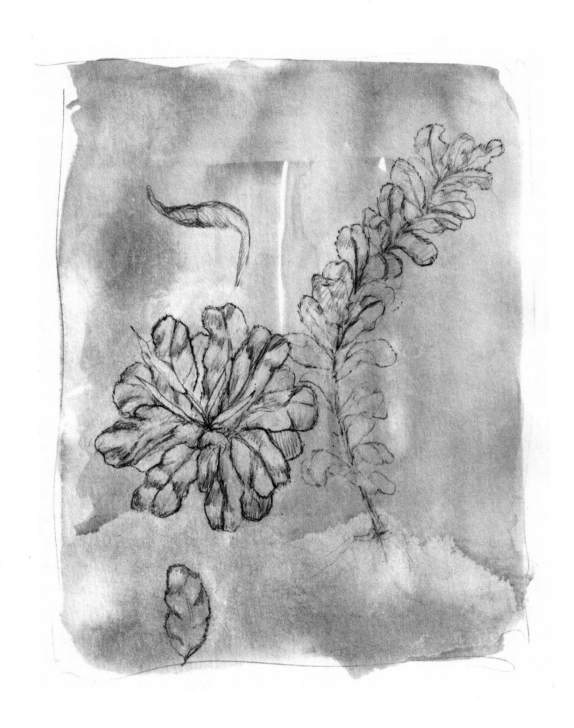

Catawba Rhododendron   *Rhododendron catawbiense*

HABITAT AND RANGE: High on ridges and mountaintops from western Virginia and Kentucky south to Alabama, Georgia, and South Carolina, with disjunct populations in the North Carolina Piedmont.

DESCRIPTION AND NOTES: In the wild the rhododendron, a large shrub or small tree, grows in dense, low-to-the-ground, nearly impenetrable colonies. It could reportedly take early settlers and explorers two days of pushing and cutting through this twiggy evergreen to cover just two miles, earning the thickets the name "hells." You may have heard the phrase "laurel hells" or "laurel slicks." This is because rhododendrons and laurels (smaller plants) often grow close together, and local people sometimes refer to rhododendron as "laurel." Further complicating matters, what is considered laurel by scientists is called "ivy" by old-timers. Rhododendron also goes by the common name "rosebay," a name more evocative of its showy, purple, bell-shaped blossoms. Rhododendrons are not seen as an obstacle these days but rather are the very reason that hundreds of scenery-seeking tourists come to the mountains in June when the flowers bloom across acres of the Smokies. In many places, this Appalachian endemic is now cultivated and invited into yards and flowerbeds.

⁓ *Michael McFee*

Please

take what's left of me, desiccated stormcloud
        of bonegrit inside a weighty bag inside a box,
up the high way to Pisgah or Craggy Gardens
        in June, when acres of Catawba rhododendron
are blooming, as they were on our honeymoon,
        their purple panoply stretched across the ridges
so dazzling our camera's film was overwhelmed,
        everything belilaced—sky, mountain, valley, us.
Carry me upslope deep into those dense thickets
        locals once called hells, near-impassable tangles
of trunks and branches and dark leathery leaves,
        lofty mazes that lost pilgrims might not escape
if not for this narrow path first blazed by bears,
        more like a stray slick creek bed than a trail.

Linger a while in that dim sanctuary, surrounded
        by coolness, inhaling the bracing peaty tang
and the faint perfume of the rose-tree blossoms
        far overhead being worked all afternoon long
by honeybees bumbling and humming their way
        into cupped flowers, the sweetest angelic buzz.
Then kneel (please) and leave what's left of me
        in that shade, safe from sun and wind and snow,
spreading my ashes at the foot of a vast shrub
        whose late spring crown is invisible as its roots
though you know it's there, a roof of brief glory
        high over me, hidden in that evergreen heaven.

HABITAT AND RANGE: Grows with red spruce at the highest elevations—as low as 4,500 feet but typically above 5,500 feet—of the Southern Appalachians, including Mount Rogers in Virginia, the Black, Balsam, and Grandfather Mountains in North Carolina, and the Great Smoky Mountains in North Carolina and Tennessee.

DESCRIPTION AND NOTES: A remnant of the Ice Age, the Fraser fir was discovered in the North Carolina mountains and named in the eighteenth century by the Scottish botanist Sir John Fraser. The evergreen is this region's version of the northern balsam fir (*Abies balsamea*). Like its cousin, it emanates the rich pine and camphor fragrance we associate with Christmas and winter holidays. In fact, Fraser fir, a staple of the North Carolina Christmas tree industry, is called the "Cadillac of Christmas trees" and has been decorated as the official White House Christmas tree more times than any other species. Maybe because Fraser fir is usually found with red spruce and, unlike the spruce, it has resin that can be "milked," early mountaineers thought the Fraser fir was the female plant of the species and red spruce the male. The two were therefore called "she-balsam" and "he-balsam," respectively. Now we know that Fraser fir (*Abies fraseri*) and red spruce (*Picea rubens*) are companion species but not of the same genus. Sadly, most mature stands of Fraser fir have been destroyed by the balsam wooly adelgid, an introduced insect first seen on Mount Mitchell in 1957. Seedlings and saplings are less susceptible to infestation than the older trees. The result on highland slopes and ridges: thickets of young Fraser firs spiked with skeletons, the stark dead trunks of a former forest.

— *Lisa Lewis*

HUSBANDRY   COMMERCE   SENTIMENT

eventually formal texts described the process of spacing seedlings
across the slopes even the slopes pierced by rock
the shallow soil fainting away still just enough for roots

how deep to dig how tall the seedlings for survival how far apart
when to fertilize to ensure adequate moisture what season what task
what measured and tested necessity

what profit what cost the cutters even inventing a performance with saws
the flourish of symmetry two hands two chainsaws the expected shape

depending on who you were and how much you thought about it
you considered it proof of the innovative attitudes of the South
that this industry emerged across the mountainsides
arranging them orderly aligning the bristling pyramids like pegs
in a puzzle or machine

or you dreamed of the long walk and the seeing and naming
the man with the notebook whose name survived him
and the nakedness of the new

though there was nothing new about the angle of human measure
its gaze swallowing cloud and trunk straight as song
many had come there and observed
if there was a difference or a change it was in guild or congress

but the sky was different neither emblazoned nor regimented
unwritten unadvertised unsold on both its legs
look there now and it's big words big concepts big money
though the peak years of the industry may not return

like driving through the night with a Fraser on the ragtop
the stump fresh cut to draw water try not to burn the house down
the landscape swayed when nobody was looking
and it made perfect sense the absolute best sense the only sense

to buy fake trees instead the same one year after year
stored in the shed or attic
and that spritz of spray or the candle Fir
spreading ghosts above everyone everything oblivion itself

the brittle past swept up like needles

Stanza - interesting form - completed thought/ moving to the next

Ironweed

Vernonia noveboracensis

HABITAT AND RANGE: Open bottomlands, low fields, and bog edges.

DESCRIPTION AND NOTES: Ironweed brings to mind old farmsteads, autumn, bottomlands, and butterflies. In late summer in Southern Appalachian wet pastures, bottoms, and boggy areas, the flowering ironweed stands tall and erect. Probably called "ironweed" because of its thick stalk and long taproot (others say because of its rust-colored seed heads), the plant's fibrous stem remains after the foliage and through winter. In the aster or composite family (note its compact heads of many small flowers), ironweed is a premier butterfly plant. From the time it blooms in late summer and fall, it is covered with swallowtails and smaller butterflies. In the fall migrating monarchs throng to it in orange clusters and sometimes overnight on its deep purple flowers.

—— *Irene McKinney*

Ironweed

Everything resists; there is iron in the roots
and the squared-off stem, silted into its deepest chambers,

and this weed stands on the slope above the dry creekbed
and refuses nearly everything. It refuses a large and showy

flower; it tried that in another life, when it was an orchid.
It refuses to be pulled out of the ground without shrieking

like a mandrake, and it refuses to let those drops
of Mary's blood ooze from its stem. In the locust tree

above it, an army of cicadas is drilling holes
in the afternoon. Each of them hoists up a pneumatic drill

between its knees. The females have an ovipositor
like a curved iron thorn; they jackhammer their eggs

into the hide of the tree. Later the damaged branches
will fall off, but they don't care. Whatever lasts

resists until it can't. Do you know what I mean?
To someone trying to grow a life, our world casts

itself in a thick iron bark. She hones herself
almost beyond belief. Exhaustion is her flower.

Oconee Bells   *Shortia galacifolia*

HABITAT AND RANGE: Acidic coves and ravines, especially under white pine and Canada hemlock in North and South Carolina along the Blue Ridge front. Planted in Georgia and other Southern Appalachian states.

DESCRIPTION AND NOTES: Oconee bells, also known as shortia or coltsfoot, is a narrow endemic. Its entire North American range fits into a circle near Lake Jocassee on the North Carolina–South Carolina state line. The plant was named for its bell-like white flowers, which appear in late March and fade to pink or lavender in April, and for its profusion in Oconee County, South Carolina. Its glossy evergreen leaves grow from horizontal stems (stolons) that clone themselves into large colonies. André Michaux first collected the plant in 1788 in what he mistakenly identified as the high mountains of North Carolina (he was actually on the Blue Ridge front in Oconee County, South Carolina). The specimen sat unidentified in the herbarium of a museum in Paris until American botanist Asa Gray recognized it as a new species. Because of Michaux's confusing location data, Gray searched for years without finding Oconee bells in the wild. It is now known to be common and colonial on the acidic slopes of Lake Jocassee and can be found blooming abundantly along the Oconee Bell Trail in Devil's Fork State Park in Oconee County. Populations in the headwaters of the Catawba River, which used to be called *Shortia galacifolia* var. *brevistyla*, are now called *Shortia brevistyla*, Catawba shortia, northern shortia, or Catawba bells. Another five or six species of *Shortia* have been identified in China, Vietnam, and Japan, evidence that species of this low-growing genus of perennial herbs probably once covered the north temperate zone from North America to Southeast Asia.

—— *Thorpe Moeckel*

As We Were, Then, on Those Steeps

> *S. galacifolia* was judged to be in a relict condition with the low incidence of reproduction sites accounting in part for its endemism.—V. E. Vivian, 1967

> In June 1760 . . . Montgomery quickly drove the enemy from about Fort Prince George and then, rapidly advancing, surprised Little Keowee, killing every man of the defenders, and destroyed in succession every one of the Lower Cherokee towns . . .—James Mooney, 1889

> A lot of plant distribution is logical; the rest is luck and history that we don't understand. —L. L. Gaddy, 2016

Runner-stem by runner-stem, the sisters
unstitched us from the duff: leaf, flower, root
      and all. June, Green Corn Moon, it was,
De ha lu yi, and we were in capsule, mute
      as ever while the two maidens bent, fingers

      still quivering, numb with numb, and tore
us up from the ground in long strands (what
      you might now call stolons), and with us
wrapped every corpse—there were a lot.
      The younger gave her father extra care:

      covered his eyesockets with our sepals,
braided dense his head with our toothed
      leatheries, filled his mouth with our tongues—
styles, pollen tubes done, song-sleuthed.
      They could smell smoke & strange metals

      from across the river beyond the confluence,
the fort's wasteful, ridiculous fires,
      but they worked as ghosts, quiet as
ghosts (though fox-screams were their eyes),
      and *Nunne'hi* guided them, those Immortals lent

      them strength of mist. Bees had spread the news.
Deer came to bed in our last dense clumps.
      To settle their guts, bear munched our leaves,
turkey, too, but not excessively (our juice
      has little taste). Scavengers, normally aloof,

      flared their wings and cocked their heads, bald
and painted, up from their rank, perfect food.
      From Spear-point's peak, Thunderbird, abuzz,
tucked & dove along the vectors of our nod.
      Even the wolves left watch of the cattle

by the fort, and slunk to the top of the cliff
and stared down the slope at the sisters
        who had woven the entire grove of us
by now around their kin. It wasn't over.
        The dead's wounds mostly hidden (not the stiff

        weight), the sisters hefted each villager,
family & friends, one by one to the stream.
        And one by one down the sisters weighed
each runner- and leaf-entwined remain
        with stones they tilted under the water,

        big stones, boulders—such was the force
of their loss. For a long time (that felt
        like none or beyond time), the sisters
worked the pool beneath the last tumult
        at *Dukus'i*, Toxaway, before the confluence—

        they waded among murmurs of light & rains
breaking on (and, more slowly, breaking)
        the stone; those falls below which some say
every beforelife's future is spoken, and one
        can know us as we are beyond the names.

Stanza / form
G gives movement to
the literal poem
in keeping with
the action described

Persistent Trillium   *Trillium persistens*

HABITAT AND RANGE: Rich woods and slopes in gorges of the Tallulah and Tugaloo drainages in Georgia and South Carolina, on the headwaters of the Savannah River.

DESCRIPTION AND NOTES: Persistent trillium is a small long-lived herbaceous perennial (some trilliums may live to be more than one hundred years old) found only in the southern Blue Ridge of Georgia and South Carolina. The small white flowers turn pink as they mature, and, unlike other early blooming trilliums, the plants "persist" late into July when the fruit sets. Although the species occurs in a few other small gorges and ravines, the heart of persistent trillium's world distribution is Georgia's Tallulah Gorge, a Blue Ridge escarpment gorge with cliffs rising up to 1,200 feet in height. Interestingly, the species was discovered downstream from Tallulah Gorge in South Carolina in the 1970s by amateur naturalists John and Edna Garst. It is often called "Edna's trillium" in honor of Edna, who saw it first and noted that it wasn't in any of her wildflower books. Persistent trillium is one of the few Southern Appalachian plants ever to be featured on a U.S. postage stamp.

— *William Wright*

Persistent Trillium

Sometimes blooms are maps of stars,
and it will be a long while before we know it.
Sometimes this trillium is kicked to marl, but survives,
a small crowd of lanterns that rupture the dark

sealed breath of the Savannah River,
where no words rise from rhododendron slopes,
down gorges of the Tallulah and Tugalo sluices.
And yet this trillium's tiny claim of land makes its own

language, delicate, certain, the river
dousing it year after year through a humus
umbilicus, a root-hymn to urge it to rise again,
to open its three glabrous eyes and steep in sun

well into July, when the sear burns
most other blooms alive. But now, under the stem,
the hem of this flower blooms dim
in the shade of the first day of spring—

the sun so slim the petals can't cling,
unlatch through the curl of this small valley
of wind, early dead and moonblown,
fewer and fewer seeding to nativity.

HABITAT AND RANGE: Calcareous rock faces, overhangs, boulders, and cave openings and moist ravines in the southern Blue Ridge escarpment gorge. Prolific throughout the tropics, rare in the temperate zone. In the United States, only in North Carolina, South Carolina, Alabama, Florida, and Arizona.

DESCRIPTION AND NOTES: A spleenwort is a type of fern, a nonflowering spore-producing plant that predates the dinosaurs and flowering plants by more than one hundred million years. Unlike most ferns, however, this small, slender fern typically has only one sorus per leaflet. (A *sorus* [plural "sori"] is a spore-packet on the underside of a fern's pinna or leaf.) In the Southern Appalachians, single-sorus spleenwort is one of several plant species of tropical origins found near waterfalls (such as Whitewater Falls in Transylvania County, North Carolina) and in other gorge microclimates below two thousand feet in elevation. It was first spotted in 1946 along the Whitewater River in Oconee, South Carolina, by Rev. A. Rufus Morgan of Franklin, North Carolina. Because of its rarity, disjunct distribution, and the alluring nature of its preferred gorge and waterfall habitat, naturalists seem to get immense enjoyment in locating this plant. As for the name, maybe, as eighteenth- and nineteenth-century herbalists claim for spleenworts generally, the tea made from its leaves *is* good for the spleen. (As a literary side note, etymologically speaking, words that end in "-wort" are ancient; the suffix has proto-Indo-European associations with "root" and was often used in names of plants considered to have medicinal properties.)

— *Gyorgyi Voros*

Single-Sorus Spleenwort

> Life has always seemed to me like a plant that lives on its rhizome. Its true life is invisible, hidden in the rhizome. . . . What we see is blossom, which passes. The rhizome remains.
> —Carl Jung, *Memories, Dreams, Reflections*

There is nothing fraudulent about this fern.
            Humble if not entirely retiring, low-lying
       but assertive in abundance, it inhabits where others
quail: limestone outcrops, lime sinks, cave openings.

Look for it (namethatplant.net tells us) *in*
            mountains' moist grottos and *near waterfalls, or humid*
      escarpment gorges, on limestone talus in collapsed sinkhole
mouths. Hobbit-lands, one might think. But no: as ferns

go, this one's neither frail, nor flowering, nor

                  fractal, its scalloped, lobe-like leaflets unrepeated

      in the leaf or in the whole or in the mass of them. Even

the charms of fiddleheaded youth, it foregoes,

providing no provender for humans. It

                grows up from the ground blunt-leaved, thin-stalked, sturdy as the

      burly, bespectacled child who, at five, already looks like

the civil servant he will be at forty

and as bluff. Dots like candy buttons children

                strip off paper line its underside. When peered at from

      beneath, these sori, veiled in white like pregnant brides, tumescent with

sporangia, reveal themselves kidney-shaped—

rumoring the plant curative, according
                    to the old Doctrine of Signatures, for spleen. Choosing
            the rhizomatic over the arborescent, it sends its
roots mat-like, map-like shallowly under soil

about which it is not that particular,
                    not even committing itself to any single
            state or continent, its diaspora scattered all about
the country and the globe—from Hawaii to

the West Indies, from the Americas (all
                    of them) to Africa, from Arizona to north
            Florida, the only place where it is rare, endangered, prized.
(As though that made a difference to the plant.) Each

hair's breadth thread of root a purchase for the next
                    and the next, the movement always sidewise, not up, no
            dendritic forkings from low to high (there were no trees back in
its evolutionary infancy). Roots

an assemblage of points, each point a place where
                    new life might emerge. How primitive to think of one's
            subterranean self entangled democratically with
kin, kith, unity in multiplicity.

Each of them is several. Frond erect, stipe
                    firm, pinnae orderly, glabrous, each stands sentinel
            on the forest floor, witness and participant. It makes no
claims, is a soldier of the ordinary.

Note: Italicized phrases in the second stanza come from the description of *Asplenium monanthes* at
Native and Naturalized Plants of the Carolinas and Georgia, www.namethatplant.net.

Tulip Poplar

Liriodendron tulipifera

HABITAT AND RANGE: Old fields, cove forests, ravines, riparian areas, and bog edges.

DESCRIPTION AND NOTES: Tulip poplar, as it is most commonly called, is not a true poplar (*Populus* sp.) but a member of the magnolia family, as evidenced by its showy clusters of green and orange flowers so beloved by squirrels and ruby-throated hummingbirds. This spectacularly tall tree (up to 190 feet, rivaled in eastern North America only by the white pine), often grows in a dense thicket of other young poplars in an old field or as a towering supercentenarian in a cove forest. Its light-colored wood ("whitewood") makes excellent barn siding, and its purple heartwood is carefully carved, cured, and polished into dulcimers and fiddles, thus the common name "fiddle tree."

—— *Melissa Range*

Tulip Poplar

Tennessee's state tree, Liriodendron tulipifera, *family* Magnoliaceae

I liked its foxheaded look, its four-peaked leaf
whiskering up at the tips; I liked
its hell-no height, so tall I couldn't reach
a branch, even with a boost; I liked it best
goldfinch bright, yellower than the ribbon
we left knotted around it all one year;
I liked penciling *poplar* in the book
I made in seventh grade, which contained
the leaves of thirty-five East Tennessee trees
and no actual knowledge of trees,
or else I would've written *magnolia*,
my fake poplar's family name—
that waxy, genteel name I like to mock.
I was proud that our state tree could grow
on mountains, in hollers, in my yard
(one dog or another chained to it),
in any shit field from one end of the state
to another, proud it wasn't soft, like moonlight
roping through branches in a habitat

imagery/ line length

only real on a TV screen.
We never used and never knew
its proper name and didn't want to know.
For my grandfather its names were *shutters,*
shingles, cabinetry; for my father
its names are the names of forty years
of dogs; for me, its names become the pulp
left in my mouth from some country club south
gracious with trees I hadn't seen and didn't want
to see. I thought it was a harder wood
than what it was because it had to be.

Wine-Leaved Cinquefoil   *Sibbaldiopsis (Potentilla) tridentata*

HABITAT AND RANGE: High-elevation rocky knobs, rocky cliffs, and crevices from Georgia to Greenland, west to the Yukon.

DESCRIPTION AND NOTES: Wine-leaved cinquefoil, also known as "three-toothed cinquefoil" or "shrubby fivefingers," has petite white flowers—like buttercups that look as if they have been bleached or blanched. It has three leaves (in contrast to most cinquefoils or "fivefingers," which have five leaves), each leaf notched into three prominent teeth at the tip. In fall and winter, older leaves of this glossy evergreen gradually turn wine red or bronze and sometimes drop off. A dwarf of the rose family, it grows usually three to four inches tall, typically in exposed rocky crevices higher than four thousand feet in elevation. Regional populations of wine-leaved cinquefoil were probably pushed south by glaciers during the Pleistocene and have survived at these high elevations in the Southern Appalachians in the last ten thousand years or so. Cinquefoils are known to contract their leaves in bad weather to curl over and protect their delicate flowers. They are also a refuge for frogs, according to nineteenth-century amateur botanist Alice Elizabeth Bacon, who observed, "the toad will be much under Sage, frogs will be in Cinquefoil."

— *Debra Allbery*

Wine-Leaved Cinquefoil

Beloved daughter, in the language of flowers,

we bow beneath the flat of the wind's hand.
Call it patience, how we hold on, how we curtsey

our aliases: *synke foul, sunkfield, shepherd's knot,*
hand of Mary. Our blossoms anonymous,
simple as a child's drawing, a cathedral window,

clutch of notched leaves in the mountain's cleft.
In another age the beloved daughters of the village
walked arm in arm before a feast day, singing:

We, cinquefoils rooted in the same soil,
buds of the same bush, let us walk together

through the stronghold. The kept secret splits its rock.

II — Mammals

American Black Bear

Ursus americanus

HABITAT AND RANGE: Black bears have historically lived throughout North America in oak-hickory forests, preferably with dense understories, though humans are now developing what was their habitat.

DESCRIPTION AND NOTES: The darkest of the bear species, the black bear is also the smallest. It measures four to seven feet long and weighs from 150 to 200 pounds. Though it's densely furred and has a strong, heavy body, it has frequently been compared to humans in folklore. This is likely because of its five-fingered feet, whose entire soles touch the ground when walking, leaving a unique print, and the way it stands on its hind legs to see farther or when threatened. The bear can also swim and climb. Its strong sense of smell—and shrinking forest lands—increasingly draw the black bear to human habitation, and it is becoming known for ripping into tents and raiding garbage. A male black bear may cover as much as one hundred miles while foraging. The bear's natural diet includes sprouts, bark, seeds, and roots; it can be 85 percent vegetarian. Black bears hibernate in winter in some areas, though in the mid-elevation Southern Appalachians where it is warmer, they sleep only occasionally and continue to forage at dawn and dusk. Look for flattened places in front of berry bushes, which may indicate a bear has stood there, feeding its sweet tooth; turned-over logs, where a bear may have hunted insects (bears' prey is mostly small scale); or claw marks on trees.

— *Mary Oliver*

Spring

Somewhere
    a black bear
        has just risen from sleep
            and is staring

down the mountain.
    All night
        in the brisk and shallow restlessness
           of early spring

I think of her,
    her four black fists
        flicking the gravel,
           her tongue

decent with the bear

like a red fire
    touching the grass,
        the cold water.
            There is only one question:

how to love this world.
    I think of her
        rising
            like a black and leafy ledge

to sharpen her claws against
    the silence
        of the trees.
            Whatever else

my life is
    with its poems
        and its music
            and its glass cities,

it is also this dazzling darkness
    coming
        down the mountain,
            breathing and tasting;

all day I think of her—
    her white teeth,
        her wordlessness,
            her perfect love.

alliteration (sonce)
form & use of white space

Deer Mouse   *Peromyscus maniculatus*

HABITAT AND RANGE: Forests and woodland edges.

DESCRIPTION AND NOTES: The deer mouse is a tiny rodent only three to four inches in length, predominantly brown with white feet and belly; a long, two-toned tail; big, round eyes; and adorably oversized ears. While storybook cute and fastidiously clean itself, the deer mouse is a known vector of Lyme disease and carrier of flu-like hantavirus, which can be inhaled as dust from dried droppings left when deer mice take refuge in barns, trail shelters, and homes. A study of deer mice in the Blue Ridge of South Carolina found that 10 percent of those sampled tested positive for hantavirus. Deer mice are nocturnal and forage omnivorously and widely from their nests, which are usually found in hollow trees, wood piles, or rocks. They are nimble climbers and can squeeze through openings as small in diameter as a no. 2 pencil.

— *Rita Mae Reese*

The Natural History of Model Organisms

> Their use in aging research is because [deer mice] . . . have maximum lifespans of 5–7 years, compared to the 3-year maximum lifespan of *ad libitum*-fed laboratory strains or wild-caught *M. musculus.*—Wikipedia

What to do when they've found a use for your life.
When they've found a use for your body? The only thing
you thought you owned.
          Is it a mistake to live too long?
Some say yes, that if you lived less
you wouldn't be in a lab,
you'd be in fields, you'd be

in those treetops you still dream about
          even after each needle.
Not one of them has erased the memory
of leaves and wind and distance and sky
though you yourself were born in captivity
and tasted none of that.

The white coats who carry in the memories
that you sniff over eagerly each morning
are no more related to you
than the deer
(another memory
of hooves and shadows)—
distant relatives,
very distant, like the planets
that still determine our fate.

The dream of treetops is a seed
slipped through the wires.
What if you're the one who loses it forever?

Some say with treetops comes talons, beaks
so better here, better you wait until the hands
find the right needle.
        Some say there is no right needle.

Some say the seed is just a seed.
Hunger makes us eat ourselves.
Some tremble with the hunger,
some as the dream arcs through them.

form → emphasis on indented lines
enjambment — lines as individual thoughts / points

Eastern Wood Rat

Neotoma floridana

HABITAT AND RANGE: Rock piles in deciduous forests. Its range, from New York to the Gulf of Mexico, overlaps with that of the lookalike Allegheny wood rat in the northern portions of the Southern Appalachians.

DESCRIPTION AND NOTES: This little rodent is also known as the "pack rat" because it makes large nests filled with objects it collects. To acquire its collections, the rat often invades woodland buildings and homes, stealing jewelry, porcelain, and even bamboo skewers and kitchen utensils. It arms the perimeters of its own nest with sharp items such as these, as well as thorny brush including black locust stems and American holly leaves. The wood rat defecates in a communal toilet (unlike woodland mice, who are not as fastidious). The species carries few diseases and is long lived (up to ten years in captivity). In the wild of Southern Appalachia, the wood rat eats acorns, berries, and seeds and drinks little or no water, like the desert kangaroo rat from the west.

— *Nickole Brown*

Self-Portrait as Eastern Wood Rat

Let us begin with my hair—
that frizzy, god-forsaken mess sprung

[handwritten: metaphor / imagery]

like Velcro from my head at thirteen, that hormone-
fed explosion of caustic fuzz that laughed in the face
of any hair goop or oil or spritz we could find
at the dollar store. It was a middle-school tease, a homeroom
landing pad for paper planes and spit wads, half-chewed
gum and gummy bears, a regular sport at my school

with one goal in mind: to make the redneck girl
in her high-water jeans cry. My hair, not just
unmanageable or *unruly* or *going through a phase* but
a real fuckin rat's nest—and that's just what my mama said,
brush in hand. This, friends, is where the learning begins,

because what I didn't know was only one rat
builds that kind of miracle nest—only one rat's a genuine
pack rat—and that rat's made for the land that gave
15   it a name. You see, I was wrong: I thought
a rat was a rat was a rat, but I should've known better

than to call similar beings all by one name, to hate them all
the same. This rat's not the undifferentiated mass gnawing
wires of red-lined neighborhoods and subway lines,
20   not those garbage-lickers that make the poor feel dirty no matter
how much they clean. No, this rat's a real forest nibbler,
wearing its growing teeth down on ground-fall pecans
and mushrooms, caching stems and roots, happy
for just what the seasons bring. And here's what I can't let go:

25   Despite the talk of rats taking over what we call
our world, this rat—forgive us—is nearly
extinct. It's our fault, working hard as we have to
pave ourselves over, our best tracts strip-mined or stripmalled,
our mountaintops literally *removed* for a vein
30   of coal, because like a mistreated girl whoring in the back
of her daddy's Chevy, it's as if we want to throw away what
we were given because we were once made to feel
it wasn't worth a damn anyway. This might be about

shame, like how I worked so hard to scrub
35   my tongue of the talk that, like me, came up
from this mud—like how I once said an old man stashing
a decade's worth of margarine tubs and dirty magazines
wasn't *a hoarder but a downright ornery cuss, a pack rat*
with his trailer-park Tupperware and tiddy magazines,
40   or how when I told mama what happened at school,
she put down the brush and quit her fussing, said, *baby,*
they're pea-green with envy is all, don't you give a rat's ass.
What I mean to say is I grew up

and figured how to shellac my hair into something
45   nearly presentable, to trick it into looking like something
it's not, but still, when I look in the mirror, it's
that little girl from Kentucky staring back. No. What I mean is

there's this kind of rat who works on a single nest all its life
and lives in that one place til it dies, just as I can't seem to quit
50 and leave this place behind, no matter how far away I move.

No, that's not quite right.
Let me say this plain: What I mean is
I once thought myself white trash—that rat
of all rats. But now I know I was only listening to the trash
55 I was told. Because a close look at the eastern wood rat reveals
a creature maybe messy and more than a little
hungry but meant to be here and still holding on, gathering
sticks and branches, broken glass and dried shit,   metaphor
crow feathers and rusted cans, wood screws and napkins
60 and candy wrappers, forgotten flannels and cassettes,
Barbie limbs and lost gloves, shreds of anything, just
anything it can find to
survive, all things sacred and profane to keep
safe and warm in a place it can call home.

Gray Fox

Urocyon cinereoargenteus

HABITAT AND RANGE: Forests and forest edges in North America, Canada to the Pacific, Central America, and south to northern South America.

DESCRIPTION AND NOTES: Silvery gray-brown to reddish brown and weighing less than twenty pounds, the gray fox may be the oldest fox species in the world. It was certainly once the only fox found in the eastern mountains. Now it competes with the introduced red fox (*Vulpes vulpes*) for food and territory, though the gray fox prefers the shelter of deciduous forests, in contrast to the red fox's more cosmopolitan range. The two are often indistinguishable in the field. The tail of the gray fox, however, is sleeker and blacker than that of the bushier-tailed red fox, may have a black stripe, and has a black tip instead of the red fox's white. What truly distinguishes the gray fox is its ability to climb trees with its catlike semiretractable claws, jumping from branch to branch and descending cautiously backward down a trunk like a house cat. During the day, it might den in a hollow tree many feet above the ground or in a brush pile or an abandoned burrow. The gray fox is omnivorous, and its diet varies by habitat. In the Southern Appalachians, it eats everything from berries and other fruit to birds, rodents, and cottontail rabbits. This feline-seeming member of the dog family typically lives near bodies of water, where, unlike a cat, it appears to delight in swimming.

⟶ *Adrian Blevins*

Fox Heart

There is no La Leche League
in the Appalachian rain forest in my heart. There is
no Gap, no Eileen Fisher, no Wi-Fi, no Dollar General.
But for five hundred million years at least there was
enough chestnut & littleleaf sneezeweed & Carolina parakeet
for everybody in the Appalachian rain forest in my heart
& in actual reality plus megatons of satiny swarms
of freshwater mussels the pearly shells of which
make good ashtrays & southern bog lemming
& woodland bison & elk—& *elk*—plus actual
passenger pigeon & certain kinds of big-eared bats
& shrews. But the freshwater mussels these days
like the wild leek & the mountain alder & the piratebush
are turning to an invisible blur in the old rivers

                              of the Appalachian rain forest
in my heart & in actual reality not to even mention
the shrimplike crayfish they'd dare us to swallow live at 4-H
to prove what hillbillies we were & how much we loved
the forest & everything already dead & dying in it.
So of course I stood there on stage in that hunting lodge
& shut my eyes to imagine the gray fox also in my heart
& in reality as the fox is one of the high priests of all this listing
by which I just mean the main gumption behind it
mostly because she's still flourishing in her sly den
with the scattered bones like a fenceline outside
since she's too busy not to be messy & far too hungry
not to sleep all day & hunt all night & too maternal
& sneaky not to steal chickens for her pups

                    & too curious not to stare at everything forever
to discern it. The gray fox can even climb trees & is therefore
also part coon & cat & I do mourn the mountain lion—
I remember as a child the bobcat's call—& do I mourn
never seeing a flying squirrel or a star-nosed mole
or a bog turtle or a diamond darter or a spruce-fir moss spider
& hate not even knowing what a hellbender is, but still
I stood there on stage in that 4-H hunting lodge
in my beloved Blue Ridge at the age of eight & shut my eyes
to call up the gray fox hiding out in a little den in the shadow
of my hillbilly heart to get the guts to open my mouth
& swallow that crayfish live so I could learn I think
to bide my time till I could sing this story of our unforgiveable sins
& try & say what a fierce little forever-thing at least our sorrow is.

North American Beaver

Castor canadensis

HABITAT AND RANGE: Rivers and streams in a wide variety of landscapes throughout most of North America south of the arctic circle.

DESCRIPTION AND NOTES: The North American beaver can weigh up to seventy pounds. (Only the South American capybara is a larger rodent.) It has a big, flat, furless tail used to slap the water and make alarm sounds. The species is also possessed of webbed feet; ears, eyes, and nostrils with membranes to protect them during long underwater swims; and oily, water-repellent fur. This fur evolved, of course, to help the beaver, but trapping for that fur nearly drove beavers to extinction in the 1800s. Now the North American beaver is common in the Southern Appalachians again. It inhabits both slow- or fast-moving water and is found, for instance, in whitewater sections of the Chattooga River (famous for kayaking) as well as human-dammed streams. Using another remarkable body part—its teeth—the beaver builds its own dams, cutting down trees and piling material up to create ponds and lodges. The lodges, in ponds or on bluffs and riverbanks, have underwater entrances to relatively dry rooms inside. The beaver's teeth are suited to its diet, which includes bark, leaves, stems, and twigs of trees and shrubs—but not fish, as some people think. Urban beavers occasionally cause flooding in parks and along roadways and so may be considered nuisance animals. In the wild, however, beaver dams and ponds create habitat for many species, dramatically increasing local biodiversity.

— *Landon Godfrey*

Landscape Painting

Two oily glazes one layered over
the other perhaps lake
madder red on hooker's green

light to produce an optical brown
the fur-mud shade formed only when seen
by the eye that desires a view

isn't wanting what makes the eye
so in painting a stack can
construct what the world looks

like as does a beaver ponding
its environs need a flood
call a beaver need a god

for moral leverage call a beaver I
don't know about that but do you
know your suspicions about reality

are well grounded the beaver
always changes everything always
I will say it again always the truth

of course is everything colors
everything but the beaver
makes it easy to see someone to blame

Syntax ?

form — no punctuation
enjambment

Northern Long-Eared Bat *Myotis septentrionalis*

HABITAT AND RANGE: Upland deciduous forests, preferably mature and uninterrupted, in eastern North America, for the most part (though populations exist in the evergreen forests of the Pacific Northwest).

DESCRIPTION AND NOTES: This bat's small body (about three inches long) is topped with ears a third of its length—nearly an inch long. Its wingspan can be more than three times the length of its body (nine to ten inches). It flies and forages on wooded slopes and ridgelines, and roosts under the loose bark of trees and in their holes and hollows. Before hibernation, in the late summer or early fall, the female of the species is inseminated. She stores sperm in utero through the cold months. Only when spring comes does she ovulate, develop a fertilized egg, then bear a single pup. Numbers of these bats have been plummeting because of the white-nose syndrome, a disease identified in 2006 that causes a white fungus to grow around bats' muzzles and is decimating bat populations of many kinds. In 2015 the northern long-eared bat was listed as threatened by the U.S. Fish and Wildlife Service. For now, these bats can still be found tucked into the cracks and crevices of caves, only their noses—and those long ears, which stick out farther than their noses—showing.

— *Rajiv Mohabir*

Northern Long-Eared Bat

As a child, I cut down
the oak in my front yard,

formed a set of runes
burned into the disks I sliced

to divine the spirits around me.
In the morning on the front porch

no twilight music. Why do I
fell what I can't imagine?

What chorus did I hack,
whose music did I gouge?

—

A historical range now curbed
            by deforestation, known for
preferring mature, interior forests,

preying with echolocation along
            ridgelines, their numbers devastated
by white-nose syndrome,

a fungus that grows on the nose
            as it crouches in a crag's seam
or a narrow hole's hibernacula.

Myotis, still, but *septentrionalis*
            their ears known to be longer
than those of smaller kin.

—

Do you hear the click of sonar
the askance assonance of a sound wave in return?

We only see the world through five
windows, imagine pinging a sonic map

from laryngeal contractions
to hear caddisfly and leafhopper-depth or

moth, frequency reflecting
flight or rest. Who calls out?

There is so much to hear,
until there is nothing.

—

Chainsaws roar
                        against trees—

Appalachia disrobes
                        green into silence.

~

Though gleaning, picking
        arthropods off leaves,
the first two hours after

sunset, long-ears prey.
       She perches in decay-
ing oaks, and as her grip

of summer loosens into
       Alabama balm, she intones,
in a series of clicks,

       chants down the sun.

~

O brown sister,
train the bone

of my cochlea
to hear the choir

of small spirituals
in echo all about.

River Otter   *Lontra canadensis*

HABITAT AND RANGE: Rivers, lakes, and beaver ponds throughout the Southern Appalachians. Prefers fast-flowing white water and clean, remote ponds. Extremely vulnerable to environmental pollution, the otter is much rarer today than it was in pre-Columbian North America.

DESCRIPTION AND NOTES: The river otter is one of the most playful animals in the region, known for sliding down banks and landing in the water with a splash for pure fun. This semiaquatic mammal's body is ideally suited for water. Streamlined yet muscular, it undulates as the otter is propelled forward by webbed feet and strong tail. Adding to its swimming abilities, the otter can hold its breath for up to eight minutes, its fur repels water, and its ears and nostrils close when submerged. The otter's nose is sometimes described as looking like a puppy's, and the otter is considered cute by almost everyone, except maybe fishermen, who might think it eats more than its share of fish. (The otter also eats amphibians, crustaceans, and mollusks.) Otters, often in families or other groups, live in series of burrows. At least one of these burrows usually has an entrance that lets the residents go straight out the door and into the water.

— *Elizabeth Seydel Morgan*

Long Mountain Otter

for Temple Martin

He is not really local, not
a Long Mountain otter—
or for that matter,
though he seems to be
smoothly furred in the curved stone,
he's neither sleek nor wet.

But he looks wet.
As if he'd slipped out of water, not
been chiseled from dry stone.
Maybe he's not a Long Mountain otter,
but an animal yet to be
named, a whole new matter.

[handwritten note: Same ending words throughout! diff order]

The *heart* of the matter,
really. In a dust-filled barn, wet
life emerges, begins to be
what can breathe, not
only in water and in air, but an otter
that takes breath in stone.

It could be a stone
from Long Mountain, as a matter
of fact, rolled to where the slick otter
slides his trout along the wet
rocks to live in the air as we do, not
underwater where he could choose to be.

It even could be
that once an otter clambered up this very stone,
forsaking the grace of water to take in the air. Not
that it matters.
It is only this stone that makes him wet.
Only Temple makes him this otter.

words!

Temple is the sculptor of the otter,
she's the one who made him be
quick and sleekly furred and wet.
In the waters of my mind the heaviest stone
swims lithely and everything that matters
moves, alive or not.

Born wet out of stone,
it doesn't matter what he's not.
The Long Mountain Otter is freed to be.

Southern Flying Squirrel   *Glaucomys volans*

HABITAT AND RANGE: Coniferous-deciduous and deciduous forests, woods, and wooded parks throughout the Southern Appalachians.

DESCRIPTION AND NOTES: The southern flying squirrel collecting nuts in a tree may not look all that distinctive. It's a ten- to fifteen-inch long rodent (including its tail) with gray-brown fur on its back. But when it spreads its legs, it reveals a creamy white underside—and a fleshy membrane, called a patagium, connecting its wrists to its ankles. Using this membrane, it can take a running jump and glide through the air. While this is not considered true flight, the squirrel's ability to steer its course by moving its legs to control the parachute effect of the patagium and using its tail like a rudder makes gliding anything but a freefall. Flying squirrel silhouettes may be seen in dawn and dusk skies as they use their large eyes, capable of vision in near darkness, to pursue insects.

— *Davis McCombs*

Flying Squirrels

Then even that falls away, the stars sizzling out
one by one and a matte-black mountain rotating hugely.
The squirrels never do not make me gasp.
I have stood in a ditch where a bullfrog slept
and watched them leap the beamwork
of our icepick thicket, catching perhaps on the wind
grave news of elsewhere, but vaulting,
I am happy to report, easily past it, over
frost curl and bluff drip, through snow's deletions,
never wholly flesh nor wholly spirit descending
the freckled limit of my flashlight's silo.
They bear like toggle bolts an improbable weight,
springing and fastening. They are glimpsed, not grasped.
They hold in their impossibility a possibility so vast.

imagery

III ～ Birds

Black-Throated Blue Warbler   *Setophaga caerulescens*

HABITAT AND RANGE: Coniferous-deciduous forests with dense understories.
Breeding territory extends from Nova Scotia south to northern Georgia. Winters in the
Greater Antilles.

DESCRIPTION AND NOTES: Small and stocky, with a drawling song: *zoo zoo zoo zheee*
("I'm so laa-zy"). The male has a striking blue head and back, white underside, and black
beak, face, and chin. A white triangular wing patch, like the tip of a pocket square (birders
call it the "handkerchief"), distinguishes both the male and the more muted female. Black-
throated blues eat bugs, including caterpillars, moths, and flies, and are known to pilfer
trapped insects from spider webs. They often nest in dense shrubs. Southern black-throated
blues—also called Cairns's warblers, after John Simpson Cairns, an early supporter of the
Great Smoky Mountains National Park—respond to calls of both northern and southern
birds, but northern birds show less interest in the mating songs of southern birds, leading
researchers to believe speciation may be taking place.

—   *Shauna M. Morgan*

Black-Throated Songs

The understory trembles
confessing the secret of her nest
in woodbine, virgin ivy.
She listens, flits her unremarkable self,
offers up a moment.

See-see-seeeee!
Shrill to a buzz,
he perches higher, bill up,
See-see-seeeee!
A melody skyward,
cotton belly, black throat quivering,
eminent plume turning blue
as the mist burns away.

imagery

See-see-seeeee! See-see-seeeee!
She vibrates her wings,
everything else falls away.

Under a deciduous canopy
hovering together in aftersongs
until the young are fledged,
until the freedom of salt air,
until the sanctuary of moist gingerlily,
until the oak and maple come again.

anaphora

There, a white spot on a wing
below the viburnum berries bursting,
a faithful warble of fruit.

Common Raven   *Corvus corax*

HABITAT AND RANGE: Worldwide, the common raven occurs in Europe, Asia, and northern Africa. In North America, it inhabits forested areas with nearby large open areas across most of the northern hemisphere, with the exception of the southeastern United States, where it is found only in the Southern Appalachians.

DESCRIPTION AND NOTES: You can distinguish these shiny, soot-black birds from crows because ravens are larger (more the size of hawks), they have heavier bills (a "Bowie knife of a beak"), and they croak instead of caw. Known for their intelligence and problem-solving abilities, these omnivorous scavengers can adapt to a variety of habitats, from their preferred mountain crags to city parks, and are an iconic, in some cases godlike, figure in art, literature, and folklore. While ravens had once all but disappeared from the region, they are making a comeback, reacquainting the Southern Appalachians with the acrobatic pivots, dives, and chases of their aerial displays.

— *Douglas Van Gundy*

Ravens

If they catch me
with my camera, they're gone.
I've always assumed

they see it as a gun
but maybe they know
it's a camera after all,

understanding the limits
the lens imposes upon them,
the inaccuracy of any image

that holds them static. Maybe
they want simply to be seen
in all their glossy black complexity—

songbirds and scavengers,
mimics and tool-makers,
at home in language

and the silence of the sky
they scissor with their wings—
or else not be seen at all.

Eastern Whip-poor-will   *Caprimulgus vociferus*

HABITAT AND RANGE: Ground and low horizontal branches in mixed pine-deciduous and deciduous woods. Eastern United States, as far west as Nebraska and Kansas, north to Canada, and south to Florida. Migrates from Florida and the tropics in spring and arrives in the Southern Appalachians in late March and early April.

DESCRIPTION AND NOTES: The whip-poor-will is also known as a "night jar"; a group of whip-poor-wills may be known as "a seek" or "an invisibility." The mottled gray and brown plumage of this chesty little bright-eyed and short-billed bird gives it exceptional camouflage in the leaf litter of its woodland habitat, where it nests on the ground and sleeps during the day. At dusk and on moonlit nights, it declares its presence (and its name) with its sharp, insistent call: "whip-poor-will, whip-poor-will, whip-poor-will." Whip-poor-wills sing more with moonlight. (A 1981 study in Georgia, "Range Expansion of the Whip-poor-will in Georgia" by Robert J. Cooper, correlates decelerating and accelerating call frequency with the diminishing and then increasing light of a lunar eclipse.) What's more, whip-poor-wills sync their egg-laying with the lunar cycle. By timing the eggs to hatch a week and a half or so before the full moon, the parents have the best light in which to forage moths, beetles, and other insects for their new young. Because of its nocturnal habits and haunting call, the whip-poor-will in folk and native lore is a harbinger of human loneliness and death. As populations are now declining steeply, however, the bird's association with omen or lament reads differently. If nothing else, its presence will continue in literature and music; whip-poor-wills appear in stories by Washington Irving, William Faulkner, and James Thurber, poems by Stephen Vincent Benét and Robert Frost, and songs by Hank Williams and Elton John.

⏤ *L. Lamar Wilson*

Whip-poor-will, I

Play dead, like you, all day, then rise at night
& sing—my throat Gabriel's genuflected cry. O
Let the souls slain at night rise first, reclaim
This desolate terrain. O let this land's redeemed
Say *No more* & drive these maniacal white ghosts
More mad. So many black & luminous smiles,
Our seek a found invisibility. Like you, I work
Now while it is night, when no white man can
Without my never-ready back. Unfurl

My ancient tongues & fill the holes in their
Sacked hearts with this terrifying refrain:
This world's all mine. All mine. All mine. All
Mine. All mine. All mine. You've lied to your
Selves. You've occupied my home too long. Get out.

Great Blue Heron — *Ardea herodias*

HABITAT AND RANGE: Swamps, marshes, lakes, ponds, and other wetland habitats.

DESCRIPTION AND NOTES: The largest North American heron, the great blue is really slate gray, with black wing tips and white wing bars. Unlike most herons, it ranges far from the tropics, nesting as far as the northern Southern Appalachians. Great blues forage in wetlands for fish and will feed year-round in the same area as long as waters remain unfrozen. Like most herons, it nests in colonies, preferring the low trees and shrubs of marshes and ponds. Standing four feet tall with a wingspan of up to six feet, this large, familiar wading bird is emblematic of wetlands in the region. Few sights are as majestic as the slow, deep wingbeats and curved neck of a great blue in flight or its motionless silhouette sentried in a swamp or creek bed.

— *Wendell Berry*

The Heron

While the summer's growth kept me
anxious in planted rows, I forgot the river
where it flowed, faithful to its way,
beneath the slope where my household
has taken its laborious stand.
I could not reach it even in dreams.
But one morning at the summer's end
I remember it again, as though its being
lifts into mind in undeniable flood,
and I carry my boat down through the fog,
over the rocks, and set out.
I go easy and silent, and the warblers
appear among the leaves of the willows,
their flight like gold thread
quick in the live tapestry of the leaves.
And I go on until I see, crouched
on a dead branch sticking out of the water,
a heron—so still that I believe
he is a bit of drift hung dead above the water.
And then I see the articulation of feather

and living eye, a brilliance I receive
beyond my power to make, as he
receives in his great patience
the river's providence. And then I see
that I am seen. Still as I keep,
I might be a tree for all the fear he shows.
Suddenly I know I have passed across
to a shore where I do not live.

Northern Cardinal   *Cardinalis cardinalis*

HABITAT AND RANGE: Forest edges, brushy understory, hedgerows, and gardens throughout the Southern Appalachians.

DESCRIPTION AND NOTES: The scarlet-plumed, black-masked, red-billed male is a common and conspicuous flash of color around Southern Appalachian woodlands and in shrubby urban and suburban neighborhoods. Because cardinals mate for life (up to fifteen years in the wild) and stay close together year-round, the brownish female is usually nearby. She builds a low cup-shaped nest, often in shrubs, out of twigs, weeds, and grass and lays a clutch of eggs—usually three or four. In lower elevations, a pair may raise several broods per year. They feed insects to their young and eat some themselves, but cardinals are primarily seed eaters and known for frequenting bird feeders. Both the males and females sing. Their piercingly whistled "cheer cheer cheer" or "purty purty purty" is often prelude to the new day's dawn chorus.

— *R. T. Smith*

Cardinal Directions

In the body of the cardinal
who hops along the tamarack limbs,
cathedrals are collapsing. Whole
worlds are falling, exhausted
stars and dialects no one left
can translate. This crested finch,
red as the last cannas
wilting, is famished. He scavenges
in a dry season for pods,
cold grubs, any scrap to sharpen
his beak or hone his sight,

and also within me the tree
of bones is giving way
to gravity, the tree of nerves
surrendering, memory's tree
releasing its leaves, though my
eyes are still seeds looking

for fertile soil, and the one bird
heavy in my chest, the cardinal
heart, still has ambitions
to forage, to sing the litany
beyond language, and fly.

Pileated Woodpecker   *Dryocopus pileatus*

HABITAT AND RANGE: Prefers mature deciduous and coniferous forests. Found through the eastern United States, on the Pacific coast, and in Canada.

DESCRIPTION AND NOTES: This remarkable woodpecker is recognized by its "kuk-kuk-kuk" call, its reverberating drumming sound, its bright red crest, and its large black and white body. It navigates with great speed, zigzagging through stands of large trees with ease. The pileated woodpecker feeds from dead or dying wood, eating large quantities of carpenter ants, beetles, and other invertebrates that it extracts with its long, sticky tongue. It also excavates nesting holes in trees, which are used by other birds in future seasons. Populations were heavily impacted by the cutting of forests in the eighteenth and nineteenth centuries. But since the twentieth century the species has been rebounding because it will live near humans or in second growth if there are some substantial standing dead trees. In the southern part of its range, the pileated was often confused with the ivorybill, now considered extinct.

— *Jim Peterson*

"Two of Them,"

I said. "Yes," she said, smiling,
"but which two?" That caught me
off guard, as her words often did.

It never occurred to me that she
5   knew specific pairs of pileated
woodpeckers, though she did spend

a lot of time walking these woods,
with and without me. We often
heard them, one answering from

10   a distance, one clinging to the other side
of the trunk of a nearby tree, its head
popping into view to check us out.

The Black Water Creek woods
must surely be an ancient home
of the pileated woodpecker.   15

We two humans hear their song
as laughter, at first mechanical
and even maniacal. But then

with listening, it isn't, containing
multitudes of subtle layers   20
all the way from raucous

to tender like singing to a lover
falling asleep forever. The field guides
call them shy, but once when we

were walking, there was a male not   25
ten feet from us on the ground, standing
atop a dead log as if he had felled it,

hammering purposefully,
cutting away bark and an outer
layer of wood to get to something   30

good, carpenter ants, scattering
wildly now in their own panicked world.
He glanced at us and cocked his head,

brown bead of an eye embedded
in a black stripe on his white face,   35
red crest a smokeless flame.

His mate called from some tree a hundred
yards away, drawing closer, until
she peered down at us from a high limb.

But a day came when there was no   40
she to *us* two, just me, and I came here to offer
her ashes to the woods. Who knew

imagery & some personification

alliteration

it was possible to love cold ashes,
and possible to know where they
belong, here, with a particular pair of pileated   45

woodpeckers playing, swooping
and swinging between the trees
overhead, working together now

as a team. A strange rain of bark
and slivers of wood fall into the dead leaves   50
all around me, among the small

white pieces of bone and ash.

Ruffed Grouse

Bonasa umbellus

HABITAT AND RANGE: The most widely distributed native gamebird. Nonmigratory. Inhabits deciduous forests in the Southern Appalachians. Alaska east to Newfoundland and south to Georgia, South Carolina, and Alabama.

DESCRIPTION AND NOTES: About the size of a crow or large pigeon, this ground-dwelling bird tends to have grayish coloration in colder climates and rufous or reddish-brown plumage further south. Other features include a short, spiky head crest, a black ruff of erect neck feathers, and a blackish band on the tail, especially noticeable on males in display. But the ruffed grouse is usually heard and not seen. The territorial male proclaims his dominion by drumming from a log, boulder, or similar perch in the underbrush, clapping its wings together in front and behind to generate minor sonic booms that sound like a distant chainsaw or motorcycle engine. This unusual nonvocal call has earned the bird nicknames of "air drummer" and "thunder chicken." When seen, usually when flushed into startlingly explosive flight, ruffed grouse can dart through the air at high speeds, dodging trees with great acumen. Its diet is famous for diversity. The grouse eats almost anything, foraging on the ground and in trees for insects, berries, leaves, seeds, buds, reptiles, even small snakes. It can also ingest bitter toxins that other birds can't and consume an impressive quantity of fibrous plant matter. It preens by "anting" (dust-bathing on anthills or in sandy depressions). Females nest on the forest floor, laying as many as twelve white eggs in well-hidden hollows scratched into leaf litter. Historically, the bird's populations have risen and fallen in predictable ten-or-so-year intervals, a little-understood oscillation known as the grouse cycle. Since the turn of the century, however, declines have accelerated, and some biologists believe that mosquitoes—and the spread of West Nile virus—are possible culprits.

— *Cathryn Hankla*

Four-Chambered Heart

Ruffed grouse, the longing in our four-chambered hearts
Was matched, when you fluttered toward me as I sat,

Beer in hand, on my deck. At first, I didn't get it.
You rounded my chair, black collar and mottled tail, imploring,

Flexing, a banty dancer in fringed leggings and mask.
Circumnavigating, fanned tail waving its coal band

Or butterflies or a waterfall, puffy neck a black planet—
You drew closer, for reasons I did not understand.

I thought my ribs quaked over nothing, but then you thrummed
For me, secreted in brush, and came a-courting.

The second day, your wings pulsed from my porch railings,
Rising in volume and complexity, finally blurring

Into love's purring engine. Hopping down to circle
My chair in practiced artistry, you hoisted your tail full sail—

My astonishment almost complete. On the third day
Of your strutting display, worry turned me sullen.

You obsessed, proud crest erect. I knew I had to go away,
Leave you for weeks. I prayed you'd find, in my absence,

A perfect mate. You argued, a-flutter and dipping and awhirl.
I tried to work it through as you entreated and swayed alone,

Almost flying at me, swerving out of tune
Before crashing back into wobbly orbit. Was I not moved

By such ardor? I hope you found her, yet I wait for
Your return. I'll never forget you, ruffed grouse,

Or your persistent drumming after what's impossible
In this world, but maybe not, in the next.

Wild Turkey

Meleagris gallopavo

HABITAT AND RANGE: Deciduous and deciduous-coniferous forests.

DESCRIPTION AND NOTES: The wild turkey is a large coppery-bronze bird with a wingspan up to five feet. Males spread and drag their magnificent array of tail feathers to get females' attention during courtship, a behavior called "strutting." The male sports fleshy red wattles on its neck and throat, a snood on its beak, and a long beard of feathers that hangs from its breast. Females are drab with no wattles but can grow short beards. Turkeys forage in groups in deciduous woods and clearings, communicating with clucks and purrs. The males' characteristic gobbling is reserved for courtship and territorial matters. Wild turkeys nest in depressions in open deciduous woods or along the margins of woodland. Unlike their domesticated cousins, they can fly.

— *Rebecca Gayle Howell*

On the Appalachian Wild Turkey
(Or, a Little Capitalist Ditty Hillbillies Learn the Hour We Are Born)

Wild means free—don't it?—to run these seedbed woods
in copperfire skins, to blend in, or a ruckus when we want,
an oracle engine too hot, too gamey, to be pinned.
But still a turkey, which to others, means *chump.* The one
free soul they see is he who has the gun; it is no choice,
to be shot erect and fed or on impossible wing, still dead.

HABITAT AND RANGE: Understories of deciduous forests, often in ravines and on lower slopes. Eastern North America, north to Canada, west to Colorado, south to Florida and Texas.

DESCRIPTION AND NOTES: Midway in size between its cousins the larger American robin and smaller eastern bluebird, the wood thrush has a white potbelly punctuated with dark spots, a cinnamon-brown back, and bold white eye-rings. The musical song of the male is unequaled in beauty in deciduous Appalachian forests, where it echoes up and down wooded ravines and slopes through late spring and summer. Its flute-like "ee-oh-lay" song seems an unending complex call-and-response of whistles and chirps. In fact, the wood thrush is actually harmonizing with itself by means of its double voice box or syrinx. The wood thrush nests in the understory and forages in leaf litter for ground-dwelling insects. Because of forest fragmentation in both its tropical winter and North American breeding grounds and nest parasitism by brown-headed cowbirds, the wood thrush has become rarer in recent years, with population declining as much as 25 percent in the past few decades.

—   *James Davis May*

Wood Thrush

Audubon put his in a dogwood,
its head arched back singing the song
he couldn't describe in words—

*I do not know to what instrumental sounds
I can compare these notes*, he writes
in aching Romantic prose.

Each song a three-part structure:
ee-oh-lay, the last part a sort of trick
duet as the bird sings two notes at once.

Field guides call the song *ethereal, haunting,*
and warn that you'll hear the thrush
before you see it, if you see it.

In Breton's *The Song of the Lark,*
a peasant girl has stopped harvesting wheat
to listen in hushed awe to the song

we must imagine by reading
her expression as she listens to the bird
that does not appear in the painting.

Five summers in the Blue Ridge,
and I haven't seen a live wood thrush yet,
though I hear them every April

singing in the grove of dying hemlocks.
Searching for them makes the song
feel as though it's without a source.

Middle of summer, the haiku
would go, *You can already hear that
the wood thrush is gone.*

They look unassumingly drab
in photographs, like small
cinnamon robins. Audubon thought

the last part of their song sounded
*like the emotions of a lover . . . doubtful
of the result of all his efforts to please.*

So much absence in art: the bird we can't see,
the song we can't describe, the autumn trees
that no longer house the song we miss.

And when the song in the painting ends?
The girl walks toward her work and draws
the sickle blade against the wheat.

[handwritten annotations in margins: "tone / voice"; "twists"; "what have I gotten out of what I've observed? poem."]

IV ~ Reptiles and Amphibians

American Bullfrog   *Lithobates catesbeianus*

HABITAT AND RANGE: Swamps, lakes, marshes, and ponds throughout the Southern Appalachians.

DESCRIPTION AND NOTES: This olive green and black amphibian lurks in most water bodies, its bulbous bronze eyes and maybe a wedge of flat head skimming the surface. The largest frog in North America (up to a pound and a half), bullfrogs eat voraciously—small birds, snakes, other frogs—and sometimes invade isolated ponds or marshes, wiping out existing communities and converting the area into a bullfrog colony. Mark Catesby, eighteenth-century naturalist and species namesake, noted that "their voracious Appetites often cause their Destruction, they being great Devourers of young Ducks and Goslins," which "provokes the good Wives to destroy them." Bullfrogs' resonant "jug-a-rum" calls intensify at dusk and continue into the morning. Males often sing in choruses to attract females, which are typically larger than males and thought to seek out the richest of these acoustic displays when searching for mates.

—— *Ellen Bryant Voigt*

Frog

can't help herself, goes in and out of water
all day long. The reed wags like a finger,
the slick patch of algae shrugs and stretches—
Make up your mind.
They have the luxury of just one life.
Frog would like to venture into the weeds, or further still,
but her skin dries, too much open air is like a poison.
Underwater, confident again, Frog
keeps her legs together
to imitate the missing tail, circles the long trout,
plunges down to sweet familiar ooze.
But Frog is always too soon out of breath
and must return to the bright element
where the other land-fish line the banks,
huge and slow, picking their teeth. Close by,
in the blurred trees, new rivals have been hatching.

Frog takes up her perch where the linked bubbles
decorate the wet hem of the pond.
She sits and sits, like a clod of grass, her eyeballs
fixed and glassy, the slim tongue uncurls, curls
in her mouth: although she cannot fly
she eats what does. And then,
staring down into her losses, into the pool
that swaddled her among her mute companions,
Frog fills her throat with air and sings.

Copperhead

Agkistrodon contortrix

HABITAT AND RANGE: Forests, woodlands, rock piles, old fields, and barns.

DESCRIPTION AND NOTES: You may encounter your first copperhead in deep leaf litter along the edge of a hiking trail. Its rusty hour-glass pattern camouflages so well with the leaves you only see it at the last moment. As an ambush predator, the snake never moves. A copperhead is a pit viper but has no warning rattles, unlike a true rattlesnake. Also, the copperhead has the least amount of venom of any Southern Appalachian pit viper; its bite can be painful, but it is rarely fatal. Although a forest species, it is often found around barns and dwellings, hunting for small rodents. The copperhead overwinters in log and rock piles or sometimes in dens with rattlesnakes. Young are born live and often have greenish or yellowish tails.

— *Jesse Graves*

Pilot

Leaves scuttle by the deer trail and my eyes
flash toward the sound, muscles clenched
as I try catch sight of the uncoiling retreat
my father and I once spotted between

slate rocks beside our creek bank.
When he chopped it with a hoe-blade,
more than a dozen babies, short as waterdogs,
spilled out and scattered into the briars.

My father called it the pilot snake,
and I imagined the quick unseen strike
of the Messerschmitt over London,
streaking red sun of the kamikaze in descent.

But I heard also an echo of Pontius Pilate,
felt the betrayal of a serpent disguised
while in plain view, holding the power
to decide death, or commutation, though

how many times I must have been spared,
gathering kindling from the woodpile, seining
minnows in the creek, digging for ancestral
treasures through the attic of the dairy shed.

Blunt copper arrow of its head, banded length
of muscle, frozen except the quivering tail,
having kept the stinging, swelling judgment
held tight within its hinged jaws.

Eastern Box Turtle

Terrapene carolina

HABITAT AND RANGE: Moist deciduous forests, especially in bogs, wetlands, and stream margins in eastern North America west to Missouri.

DESCRIPTION AND NOTES: The box turtle is a familiar sight in the Southern Appalachians, often spotted crossing roads after spring and summer rains. It hides out during winter, burrowed into soft, damp ground. This terrapin has a hinged plastron, which is to say, its brownish yellow-orange shell has a doorlike part it can close, retracting its body into a "box." For all the protection a shell provides, there are some drawbacks: During mating, a shell is cumbersome, and a male has a good chance of ending up flipped on his back. If he cannot right himself, he can die like this. The male can be distinguished from the female (even when not in such a compromised position) by his bright reddish eyes and concave lower shell plate. The box turtle often lives twenty-five to fifty years and can live even longer. In the last few decades, the box turtle has become rarer, probably due to land development and its being collected to sell as a pet.

— *Deborah A. Miranda*

Eastern Box Turtle (*Terrapene Peregrinus Temporalis*)

They meet on the mountain, carrying orange, yellow
and black calligraphy through October rain.

Male and female, elastic necks stretch out in prehistoric
passion beneath silvery leaves: concave lower plate

presses against carapace. Puzzle pieces, twin halves,
they've roamed the underbrush looking for this *yes*.

Her tail sweeps to one side, his rear plastron lowers,
back legs link. Lust holds them steady; claws rake top shell,

carve wet red clay. Topaz eyes dazzle like tiny suns.
Their hunger persists on convoluted ridges of oak and pine,

cedar and alder; endures separate solitudes under thick
wineberry and blackberry vines; navigates granite slabs,

a creek wandering through whole galaxies. Beaks bite,
shells crack—this is no tame lovemaking—the male rises

on the stiff back edge of his shell, thrusts in slow motion.
It's late in the season, but female turtle, old soul, survivor,

makes of herself a living time portal; stores her mate's seed
in her body's secret compartment. All winter, she'll hibernate

inside a hollowed-out space in the heart of the forest. By spring,
her mate may be far away, mounting some other fiery sister.

It won't matter. When she is ready, this small mountain
of a mother will unfreeze time, let egg and sperm rendezvous.

In the saddle between Big House and Little House Mountains
she'll dig her nest on a humid summer night. In due time,

small slow pilgrims will plow their way out from the earth—
each hatchling choosing a direction, each soul setting off to scale

what can't be scaled. Each shell bearing black brushstrokes:
a scripture of blessings for traveling through time.

Love!

Eastern Hellbender   *Cryptobranchus alleganiensis*

HABITAT AND RANGE: The hellbender is almost an Appalachian and Cumberlands specialty, but there is also a subspecies in the similar environment of the Ozarks. Look for hellbenders in clear, unpolluted, swiftly flowing rocky streams of medium size.

DESCRIPTION AND NOTES: With a maximum length of nearly thirty inches, the hellbender is one of the world's largest salamanders (though it is surpassed in size by relatives in China and Japan). The creature is impressive, but it is perhaps not conventionally pretty. It has a large broad head (mostly taken up by a wall-to-wall mouth), tiny beady eyes, and skin that drapes in folds, looking like a suit three sizes too large. The excess skin is important in that it functions as an auxiliary lung, taking up oxygen through blood vessels close to the surface. The unattractiveness is enhanced by the slimy texture—hence the unflattering name by which it is also known: "snot otter." Yet if you ever have the chance to watch an active hellbender, the fluidity of movement may well remind you of an otter. Today the hellbender is in trouble because of dams, pollution, and sedimentation but also because of misplaced fear. More than a few hellbenders have been killed when unintentionally captured by fishermen. On the other hand, a growing hellbender conservation movement includes efforts such as the strategic placement of large flat rocks in streams as hellbender housing. The rocks are used not only for refuge but also as safe places that will guard the large, transparent, gelatinous egg masses the hellbender attaches to them.

— *Ricardo Nazario y Colón*

Hellbender

Sweet water body, breather of nighttime air
when it's best to conjure up food from bed of springs.
Guardian of rivers, coal mine Canary from under
the flatness of river rocks, known only to black-tail deer.

Named by fork tongue Mud devil. Propelled by four tiny
feet and a flattened rudder tail. Moves steadily beneath
the glimmer of a starry sky. Grand master of chess,
proficient hunter is this giant salamander.

Rare and elusive, glassy eyes set wide almost shut.
Its skin slimy, detects lights and shadows. Elongated
form like rafts undulates over foam covered rocks.
This gatherer of aquatic smells was summoned by God.

Eastern Newt

Notophthalmus viridescens

HABITAT AND RANGE: Wet or moist woods. Canada south to Florida, west to Minnesota and Texas.

DESCRIPTION AND NOTES: The greatest chance to see the eastern newt—one of only seven newt species in North America—is on the hiking trail in summer when you may run into a juvenile of this creature, the red eft. This five-inch-long reddish-orange amphibian is what a newt looks like in mid-life. Before adolescence, the newt is an aquatic, feathery-gilled larva or tadpole. After a few years' terrestrial jaunt as an eft, the eastern newt reverts to a grayish green and becomes a spotted aquatic adult, returning to the water to breed in complicated courtship rituals during which males release pheromones and wiggle and fan-dance their tails. All three stages of development may take more than a decade, as the eastern newt can live up to fifteen years. Its long life is due in part to the presence of a toxin that makes it unpalatable to fish and crustaceans such as crayfish.

—— *Laura-Gray Street*

Life Cycle of the Eastern Newt
A Love Poem

Fierce, the fire-lit membrane of red eft in our path
that day. Our first date-hike on the A.T., you finding,
feeding me wild blueberries and explaining how
"eft" and "newt" are really the same,
                            that "an eft"
(variously an *eute* or *ewt(e)*) was misheard and misread
as "a newt," and then split into separate references—
eft for the wandering, terrestrial adolescent, *newt* for
the aquatic adult homing ferromagnetically to vernal pond.

In linguistics, it's called juncture loss, or rebracketing,
the colloquial blurring of word boundaries.
                            Nearsighted,
I squint to see a smeared world shapeshift, like words
thatwereoncewrittenalltogether thawing from medieval
manuscripts and realigning,
                    the way time has spliced
the two of us since a trail blaze phased us into marriage.

The Eastern newt can live for 15 years. I want to think
our very own eft is still out there (like we here), softer,
submerged, dimmed to waterlogged green, just a spackle
of vermillion to vouch for the poison it brandished
in a drier life

            and keeps cached for emergencies. But
that newt, changeable, interchangeable one among
throngs, is surely gone, as so much is gone, and going.

We concede that neither of us perceives the other
clearly, without projection or distortion,

                                  but we can fix
on salamander red; search for the eft, sharp as a fresh
gash, at every switchback juncture, with each loss
(species, loved one, appetite, habitat, memories, direction,
memory, home).
                What we encountered on a trail through
Blue Ridge spruce and hemlock existed solidly beyond
us. It spawned in us something amphibious we still find
both consoling and indigestible.
                         So I won't end here, not
with elegy only. The eft/newt has a defense mechanism,
the unken reflex. Threatened, it arcs head back toward tail,
flashing its toxic-warning undersides.
                          Red being ubiquitous
code for danger, do not trespass, I dare you to feed on me.

Northern Slimy Salamander   *Plethodon glutinosus*

HABITAT AND RANGE: Moist deciduous forests, under leaf litter, logs, and rock piles throughout the Southern Appalachians.

DESCRIPTION AND NOTES: If you ever pick up a slimy salamander, the experience will stick with you. That is, your hand will be covered in a sticky substance that takes several days to wash or wear off. Hence the species' other common name, "sticky salamander." The salamander's secretion is a defense mechanism against predators—none want a mouthful of slime—though the salamander itself is a predator of small insects. The skin, which is streaked with silvery blue and scattered with spots, also has a surprising function: the salamander breathes through it instead of using lungs. More than forty kinds of lungless salamanders, or plethodontids, are found in the Southern Appalachians, which has more species of this genus than anywhere else in the world.

⁓ *Dan Stryk*

Slimy Salamander

Each weekend, after work & cluttered duties of the town,
        we leave it all behind
                to walk, in silent humor,
                                        to the heap
of rotting lumber—in the "mud-bowl"
            by the swampy woodland river
        where It lives.

Each time we jest It's the same one, waiting
        there, aware of our approach,
                            appraising
the spiritual worth of our buried week
        in Its small, but subtly wise,
            amphibian brain . . .
                                        To *then*
grace us with the dazzle of gold speckles
        on black slime,
                grinning up

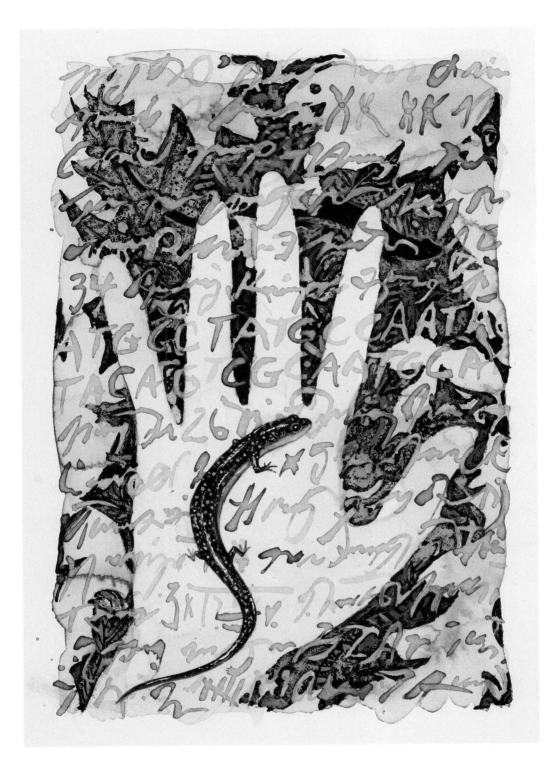

125

like an old friend
with milky bubbles
of Its knowing eyes.
Or sometimes—
if we've failed Its test—fading into emptiness
of mud, dead leaves, & chips
of bark,
as swiftly, in deep silence,
we stoop down . . .
to flip the log—

where It waits for us / or doesn't,
meaning we're *aware* /
or *dull*—to learn our spiritual place
in the Here & Now.

So each week we visit It:
to seek Its vision
of our passing lives—to play, "for mortal stakes,"
our Spiritual Game.
Believing,
"absolutely," in Its *presence* / or Its *absence*,
which we gaze upon, with humor, as a *blessing* /
or *sage curse* . . .
To stir our
weary visions to *Its Vibrance*—like a beacon—
through the coming murk & litter

of another cloudy week.

Painted Turtle   *Chrysemys picta*

HABITAT AND RANGE: Common in beaver ponds, natural oxbows, and artificial lakes in the Southern Appalachians. One of the most widely distributed turtles in North America, from Nova Scotia and Quebec south to Georgia and west across the Great Plains to the Pacific.

DESCRIPTION AND NOTES: In late March or early April in the early afternoon, bubbles appear on Southern Appalachian beaver ponds. A small "painted" turtle head appears above the water's surface, then the body. Two days later, hundreds of turtle heads bob on every pond. Winter is over; spring is here. The painted turtle, like the spring peeper, is a harbinger. A striking creature with a red underbelly (plastron); red- and yellow-striped legs, head, and neck; and a colorful back (carapace), the painted turtle grows four to ten inches in length. It eats almost anything it can find in its native pond. Rarely seen out of the water except during egg-laying, the painted turtle burrows into the mud of the pond bottom in fall and overwinters there by lowering its metabolism to a minimum sustainable rate. In northern climes it probably spends more of its time in the mud than in the sun, but in the Southern Appalachians painted turtles can be seen basking in ponds and lakes all but a few months of the year.

— *Lisa Kwong*

Letter to the Female Painted Turtle

You make mating look so easy: be
pursued, engage in a tango of red and yellow
striped limbs, then sink to the bottom of the pond, rest
in soft mud, let him mount you with his carapace. He leaves.
If only human leaving was so simple: we could let go
without snapped heart threads and abandoned rings
once desire dries up like hard, cracked mud.
I envy your freedom. Do you ever wish
you could chase him instead when he turns
to face you, claw-caressing your head, slapping
your forelimbs like human children playing a schoolyard
game? If this touch zigzags lightning through
your shell, you stroke him back. Do you care
about choice, or do creatures of your world not worry

about emotions and violence? Perhaps he wasn't your choice,
but he can leave, and you will nest, lay your eggs, also leave.
You'll bask solo in the sun, eating earthworms
until your small beak drips with abundance.

Spring Peeper   *Pseudacris (Hyla) crucifer*

HABITAT AND RANGE: Margins of shallow wetlands such as marshes, beaver ponds, and ephemeral pools throughout Southern Appalachia.

DESCRIPTION AND NOTES: This frog's call—often compared to sleigh bells or birdsong but truly distinctive—is the harbinger of spring in eastern North America. It is a tiny creature (an inch long), and its individual voice is high-pitched, with a fragile quality. Since it sings with thousands of others of its kind, however, their combined chorus can be heard from a mile away or more. In March and April, choruses begin at dark and often continue until midnight, as spring peepers seek mates. Only the male calls. The female, after she has bred, lays clusters of nearly a thousand eggs near the water's edge. The frog stays close to water—and to the ground, though it has toe pads for climbing and was long classified as a tree frog. The spring peeper can be distinguished by the cross or *X* on its back. (*Crucifer* in its scientific name means "cross-bearer.")

—— *Robert Morgan*

Peepers

The choral outcry by the pond
one final winter afternoon
sounds less like little peeping chicks   Sound
than scream of some far-off alarm,
as though a locked door had been sprung.
But what do peepers glimpse from pool
and marshy bank and weed and brush
or willow branch? Do they foresee
the coming weeks of fertility
and rampant mating in the mud
and eggs laid by the myriad?
Or do they look ahead to drought
and winter cold and warn themselves
and all who hear of gulping fish
and salamander, preying bird
and foraging squirrel, the certain end
of summer's procreative binge,
foretelling frozen pond and grave?

Or do they simply celebrate
the moment, seize the day they have
with melancholy song of love,
as humankind are known to do?

Timber Rattler   *Crotalus horridus*

HABITAT AND RANGE: Throughout Appalachia and beyond to the south, north, and west. Prefers forests, forest edges, and rock outcrops.

DESCRIPTION AND NOTES: The timber rattler is *the* rattlesnake of eastern North America. Two color phases of the snake exist: the yellow (or brown) phase and the black (or gray) phase. Mountaineers used to say that yellow phase rattlers were females and the darker phase serpents were the males. That's incorrect. Black rattlers are more likely to be found in the Blue Ridge and yellow or "canebrake" rattlesnakes in the coastal plain. However, their excellent camouflage makes them hard to spot in any woods habitat. That's where the famous rattle—a set of scales on the tail made of keratin, like human fingernails—comes in. The snake shakes the rattle to make a vibrating warning sound. Its venom, delivered by hypodermic teeth that swing down on hinges from its jaw, is extremely poisonous, but despite tales from bar rooms and general stores about monstrously huge snakes, the rattlesnake grows only up to nearly five feet in length and five inches in diameter. (And while we're dispelling myths: the practice of counting the rattles to determine a snake's age is also inaccurate, according to herpetologists.) The rattler rarely strikes large mammals such as humans, preferring rodents and smaller creatures. One of its lesser-known but interesting characteristics is heat-sensing pits on either side of its head. These pits are why it is referred to as a pit viper and how it can sense prey, or you, coming its way.

— *John Lane*

Crotalus horridus

When I need relief
from being only human
I meander upslope, scout
the stone lookout tower,
edged with brittle morning
sun and conjure a rattler's
bright coils. It's an old presence
I feel there with every step
into laurel slicks or onto vague
trail verges. On the mountain
the ground itself is shot
through with native venom.
Rattlesnake plantain grows

too thin to hide sunning
buzz-worms. It takes Galax for that,
especially along the ledge trail
where they sometimes den
with copperheads. Darkness
runs deep in those forgotten
shadow caves. Old-timers say
the devil himself twisted
slumbering pairs of black-tailed
timbers to forge the gates
of hell. In their presence
I seek salvation, a blessing.
I look behind rotting hemlock
logs, stepped across not out
of fear, but knowledge one
might linger there in supplication
and, once sighted, anoint
me with its sizzling wildness.

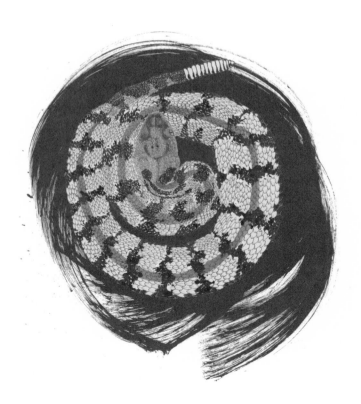

V ~ Fish

Brook Lamprey

Ichthyomyzon greeleyi

HABITAT AND RANGE: There are up to five species of lampreys in the Southern Appalachians, the most widespread being the mountain brook lamprey. This lamprey lives in the Mississippi drainage all along the Appalachian mountain chain in clear gravely streams or muddy backwaters but not larger rivers.

DESCRIPTION AND NOTES: A brook lamprey spends as long as seven years blind, buried in mud, feeding on what it can filter out of the muck, looking like a worm. After developing fins and eyes, the little lamprey emerges, only to find that its digestive tract has degenerated and its mouth converted to a sucking disk, suitable for picking up rocks to build a spawning nest. It reproduces in a great swarm and, purpose served, lives at most three weeks as an adult. The brook lamprey should not be mistaken for a parasite; it does not use its disk-mouth for sucking the blood of live fish, as the sea lamprey does. What it does share with other lampreys, as well as with rays and sharks, is a special characteristic: a spine of cartilage rather than bone. This feature excludes the lamprey from the ranks of the vertebrates, including mammals, birds, reptiles, amphibians, and "true" fishes. Regardless of whether they are "true" or "higher" fishes or whether people find the way in which their brief life is spent appealing, lampreys have existed for millions of years.

— *Catherine Carter*

Mountain Brook Lamprey
Ichthyomyzon greeleyi

Lambere, to lick, *petra*, stone.
Among your own, you're lambent,
flickering, licking creek floors like old-
gold tongues or slender fingers;
secretive stone-sucker, your larvae
light dim mucus-tube lamps
in the silty ooze below the rapid riffles.
Sand-eater, algae-skimmer,
ecosystem engineer filtering and tilling
bright air into streamy substrates,
you're no parasite
like your great sea-going kin;
you lack the cachet of horror,

lack even the jawless mouth-
gear, the grating teeth, until you
change—and then, adult, you don't eat
at all, let alone drink blood.
Your tiny hagfish maw
clutches only stones, shaping
shallow nests for your spawn;
maturity is only for love, brief
delight sliding over into death
easy as a lamprey
through water, as light through glass.

And none knows your numbers,
or what *stream* will mean
when they're dammed into zeroes
round as a buccal funnel.
Secret-keeper, that rasp-
file mouth shapes no sound,
tells us nothing. If you go,
you'll go with no word,
sucking at the stone
of silence as if it held all secrets,
all the slippery lives past and to come.

Chucky Madtom

Noturus crypticus

HABITAT AND RANGE: May once have occurred more widely but is now known only from about one and a half miles of Little Chucky Creek in Greene County, Tennessee, where it was discovered in 2005.

DESCRIPTION AND NOTES: The chucky madtom gets the first part of its name from the Nolichucky River watershed (not any Charles). The "mad" part comes from a unique weapon it wields: a poison gland at the base of the pectoral spines which delivers a feeling like a bee sting. The madtoms are a group of miniature catfish (genus *Noturus*), which could easily be taken for the young of the more familiar large catfish. The largest *Noturus*, the stonecat (*Noturus flavus*), may grow to a foot long, but most of the approximately twenty-five species are truly diminutive (under four inches long). If you have a tiny catfish in hand and want to know if it is a madtom—without getting stung—you can look at the adipose fin on the back between the dorsal fin and the tail. (The adipose fin is really a tab of fatty tissue without the rays of spines expected from a fin.) If it connects to the tail, you have a madtom. If it's freestanding, your fish is a catfish that is still growing up. Chances of finding a chucky madtom should increase in the future because Conservation Fisheries, Inc., in Knoxville, Tennessee, with the support of many conservationists, is breeding more of the species for eventual reintroduction into streams from which they have been eradicated by pollution and deforestation.

— *Holly Haworth*

Through the Burning World You Blazed

Found, new madtom species, 2005. Herein described.

What's that
mad little shadow
beneath the riffles
that curl in like pockets?

Lurks in rock-slab crevice,
sinks into its scaleless gossamer skin,
seeks not the spotlit surface of silv'ry seens.
Its eyes' coinage the smooth distillate

lots of unknown —
so voice of narrator
asking fish

10 of light that pools at the bottom,
it puffs not up its swim bladder—
but let us not call it bottom-dweller. Not "it." *You*, fish:
magician. I'll call you *Noturus crypticus*.

Distribution: Greene County, Tennessee. Two-mile stretch of
15   *Little Chucky Creek, from the mouth of Jackson Branch*
to the Bible Bridge road crossing.

What trick, this evolutionary
blip of creation. You've written your existence scriptless
among the benthic all these years,
20 carved out a life endemic,
your kind in one lone creek-corner
of the world's wide waters.

Unknown diet, spawning times, predators.

What rituals
25 do you enter there,
among the Bigeye Chub, Central Stoneroller,
Stripetail Darter, Striped Shiner, and Banded
Sculpin? What other shadow do you fear,
what roils your cold blood an octave? Your
30 barbels skimming gravel, among the soft nymphs
of mayflies or armored ones of stone-
flies, among the encased wriggling larvae of caddis,
what do you delight upon?
And what precise tilt of the earth's axis
35 urges your secret heart to fire and spawn?

Can be assumed species nests under stones like all other madtom species,
males guarding eggs and larvae three to four weeks.

Once spawned—the female having spewed her eggs,
male sputtered his seed into each globe (we must guess,
40 based on genus, else what shall we tell of you?)—

Mr. Madtom, you build a temple,
seal yourself with the eggs,
close openings off. Circling inside
that crypt of stones, pectoral fins
45 sweeping out like a robe, you supplicate yourself
to the slow surge of life.
Bend to listen into the translucent orbs.
Tending to each as a prayer, you starve yourself
and wait while the missus dances her eggless skeleton
50 into ecstasy in the currents;
you rest, a cessation—
feel those specters of future larvae
squirm to come to form.

There hidden you dwell: in completion
55 or what subtle action of multiplication.

Distinguished from other madtoms (genus Noturus) by anal fin, and by pigmentation.
mtDNA showed lineage independence.

These stones were alchemists
three and a half million years ago
60 or who knows when
your copper splotches
became fused with birch-leaf pigment
at the pectoral and dorsal or when
your anal fin radiated outward
65 two more rays (eighteen of them)
to become three-quarters of a wheel
almost spinning from the spine of your tail
and when if given the veering chance
you might have become the sun itself.

Only fourteen specimens collected; none recently found. Last known specimen perished in hatchery aquarium awaiting a mate; intended breeding program failed.

You double-helixed stroke of luck,
I am losing the use for your name
75 soon after I've named you,
you cryptic flicker of language.
My tongue plies the silence of eons
like your dorsal did the bedrock waters.

And when did the tense of you shift?
80 (Or has it yet?— foolish hope I hold onto.)

Presently, *crypticus*, you are a screen of smoke
at the bottom of the creek
behind which lies a vault of silt
that is inside a basket of nothing but stones and crawfish
85 or nothing, only rubble.

I turn a rock slab over. Like a gray sky
it tilts; underneath, there is no trace
88 of a comet.

allusion
imagery
→ form
   ↳ stanza based on
      writing of
      allusion
   ↳ voice

HABITAT AND RANGE: This Mississippi drainage species was once so affected by manmade pollution and dams blocking spawning that none were documented in Appalachia between 1946 and 1992. But in 1992 hatchery-bred lake sturgeon were successfully reintroduced to the upper Clinch River, and the effort was replicated in 2015 in the French Broad. Now this primitive species is slowly resuming its place in the Tennessee River Basin, where it has lived for an estimated 135 million years.

DESCRIPTION AND NOTES: "Horsing in," a phrase used to describe a panicky angler who dispenses with the niceties of playing a hooked fish, instead trying to bring it in by force, derives from the possibly apocryphal tale of using draft horses to haul white sturgeon out of the Columbia River in the Pacific Northwest. The sturgeon found in Appalachian watersheds isn't as big as the white (which can weigh as much as 1,285 pounds). Nor does it produce caviar as the Russian beluga sturgeon does. But this fish, with its upturned snout and body covered with bony plates, snuffling along the river bottom in search of mussels and crustaceans, is still interesting. Its swim bladder was the original source of isinglass, used in clarifying beer. It can be as long as nine feet in length and weigh more than three hundred pounds, making it overwhelmingly the largest fish native to its region. And the lake sturgeon is also a big deal because—even though it doesn't begin to reproduce until it is at least 14 years old, spawns only every 3 to 12 years, and has a life-span of up to 150 years, meaning none of us can plan on fishing for it in our lifetimes—people are working to reintroduce it. In this way, the species functions as an indicator of improving water quality—and good human qualities.

⌒ *Sean Hill*

Lake Sturgeon

When you think of fish, if you think of fish,
do you think of this fish? If so, do you think
of a dish of caviar or the Civil War?
                                   For me this fish brings
            to mind an elbow or knee, places we bend
            where touch is close to the bone. Touch
your patella—from the Latin for a "small shallow dish,"
and this one upside down and covered, skin over bone plate—
you get close to the feel of sturgeon with its rows of scutes

(starting more like "skew" than "school" and ending like "boots"),
bony plates under their rough brown skin.

Since these drab late bloomers don't mate
till their teens or even twenties and then only
every three years or so, do you think *stodgy
sturgeon*? Do you know our appetites took
their generations before they could be?
       Their roe fed an economy
for a time in the late nineteenth century.
                    These somber bottom feeders
are long-lived fish. The males live into our middle-age;
the females can live to be one hundred and fifty or so
        —twice our lifetimes.

If fish could talk, I would settle in with one of these
antique Tennesseans and ask
            *If fish had knees, when you were a fry
      at your father's how did he explain to you the cries
         of men at the Battle of Chattanooga,
           the thud of bodies come to rest, the boot-thump
           of rough brogans, the report of rifle and cannon fire
      —Southern men* (not bending the knee to keep others
in their thrall, claiming generations before they could be,
using slave labor to feed the economy) *routed on the ridges
above your home?*
               What rippled your sky?
                      Did you hear

    *cannon fire for thunderclap
and wait for rain?*

That's what I would ask,
if fish could talk,
and I could find one
that survived the last century
in those Southern waters
we dammed and sullied.

Mottled Sculpin   *Cottus bairdii*

HABITAT AND RANGE: Scattered throughout North America. In many of Southern Appalachia's rocky streams, it is the single most abundant species, sometimes accounting for a majority of all fish at sites where there may be twenty total species.

DESCRIPTION AND NOTES: The mottled sculpin is a predator with an enormous mouth that preys on aquatic insects, crayfish, smaller fish, and fish eggs. This fish dominates by thriving at the bottom of streams. It spends much of its time on stream floors in crannies among rocks or using its huge pectoral fins to travel along the bottom with a movement much like walking. (The swim bladder, which allows fish to control their buoyancy and thus the level at which they float, is reduced in size in this species. That means the sculpin can't stay at the top of the water long—that's not its natural place—just as we can't stay suspended in the air when we jump.) The mottled sculpin used to be known by a more colorful vernacular name in Appalachia: "mollycrawbottom." As fewer children play in creeks and fewer people capture fish for use as bait, familiarity with natural surroundings is lost. With it, the associated local vernacular diminishes. But mollycrawbottom—or, as it is known in other variations in other areas, the "mosshead sculpin," "frogmouth sculpin," "warty sculpin," "fluffy sculpin," "spineless sculpin," "belligerent sculpin," and "grunt sculpin"—abounds. An adage among biology students in the region is that "where there's a rock there's a sculpin."

⟶ *Kevin McIlvoy*

Thank You For

acknowledging that all your senses, all your heart, all your mind comes alive in response to the small badass bucket-eye creature of mine you have rejected—pugnacious-looking mollycrawbottom (no larger than your wet thumb or your cauliflower ear, no smaller than your dry prick) partnered in a dance with the algae-stained river stones upon which it licks at tasty flecks that slip-streaming sunlight formed, while enclouding itself in Paleozoic silt by circular tail-flicking and fin-flexing shuffling promenades shaming mere ballets of swimming. I should not have sent it to your publication, small hospice aquarium.

In the currents above mollycrawbottom, the speeding traffic of hatchery rainbows muscles untamed old Appalachian browns to exit lanes and into streams and under crumbling cutbanks on poison-crusted agricorporate land. Still, in the collapsed arteries of the watershed the mesmerizing calming beings creep-swim. River guides call them "bad first drafts of baitfish," and field biologists say they are "easily mistaken for rifle shells or discarded triple-A batteries." Before the age of reason, every child draws this same womb-fresh swimmer from dream-memory, pool and riffle and releasing world in one body with vague margins. You have had no niece, nephew, no children, grand or great, no childhood, then?

You with your fine-mesh small-net hearts, with your search engines replacing your instincts, with your necks stiff from self-sniffing, what species do you assume will outlast the most recently dismissed? What species will endure despite you, what inedible crawl-bottom prose poems too unchangeable to be replaced?

I am sorry to learn that you do not believe readers would find this underworld aliveness enough.

I will now wander again into the woods where rustling dead saplings despoiled rank nests bitter-tasting fruits where singing-flying seeds drumming fragrant rains & & & fantastical frog hordes rough-lusting in puddles are all always always have been "all too complicated for a sufficient number of readers to relate to."

Respectfully,
The Author

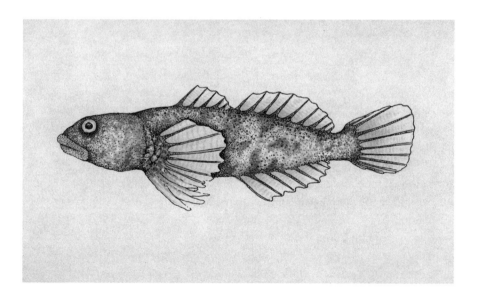

Sicklefin Redhorse

HABITAT AND RANGE: Endemic to the Little Tennessee, Tuckasegee, and Hiwassee watersheds in North Carolina, Georgia, and Tennessee.

DESCRIPTION AND NOTES: The once-abundant redhorse was probably the principal fish captured in the ancient Native American fish weirs. By contemporary standards, the redhorse can still be numerous and, due to its size, occurrence in shallow water, and appearance, it is among Southern Appalachia's most observable fish. Redhorses school in large groups and have large scales that are clearly distinguishable at a distance. Also, the fish's red fins, which are hooked or sickle-shaped, are noticeable if they break the surface. Yet the sicklefin redhorse was undocumented before 1992. More than one observer had commented on how an occasional redhorse from the Little Tennessee had an elongated first ray on the dorsal fin. But no one had differentiated it from the other five species of redhorses in the river until Bob Jenkins of Roanoke College. The sicklefin has yet to be assigned a scientific name, hence *Moxostoma* sp. ("sp." for species, essentially a placeholder while the formal process of description and publication unfolds). The common group name "redhorse" refers to the color of the tail and dorsal fin and perhaps to a "horsy" quality of the *Moxostoma* face. As for "sucker," which, along with the phrase "bottom feeder," is used pejoratively, it may not be a fair representation of the fish. Most suckers require clean, relatively sediment-free water to thrive. Yes, the sucker's face functions like a vacuum cleaner, but this is a useful feature for siphoning insects and other small organisms from cracks and crannies.

— *Janisse Ray*

Sicklefin Redhorse

From the lower reaches of Burningtown,
from Iotla and Forney, Deep and Hanging Dog,
they are a school of red horses
galloping up the mountain streams.
5 For thousands of years they have plunged upward
toward the future, and still they push
against swift waters, centuries eroding behind,
loss crashing and breaking over.
I will not stand in sorrow as long
10 As they need me to stand.
I will climb onto the bridge at Reliance
and watch them as they pass,

taste of dried fish bones like granite flakes,
junigihtla, silt in the mouth,
15 red feathers dancing, horse beneath me,
pot of heavy bones.
I am carried away.
Yes, my brother too is dead.
Yes, when we gather before a fire
20 our house is divided, eroded, small.
Is there a list where I can write
my feast of casualties, as we chase the ages
into a stone weir and gather them?
My baskets are heavy with stones
25 and the rock is coppery, brassy.
It glints and leaps, tails flying.
The rock fills my eyes, mouth, belly.
And yet they come, tumbling through
rushing waters, smoothing the edges of time,
30 out of the Tuckasegee, the Hiawassee
and the Oconaluftee, a herd of stones
spilling into the deep pools of their breeding,
so many the red feathers
make the rivers burn, fire-water, boiling stew.
35 I see the floating lilies of their eggs,
diaphanous veils and mists, the sacred female,
stallions waiting with the gift of seed.
Because the first responsibility of the son
and the daughter is to return.
40 I see the ancestors coming down
with their baskets, the girls laughing on the
silver-wet boulders, the young boys thigh-deep
in the rushing cold waters wrestling the wild red horses
the way boys will do. Corrals full of stones.
45 Streams of tears. Years eroding from the old mountains,
their words filling my ears:
amaganugogv, soquili, aninvya.
I see my brother fishing from the thickets of rhododendron.
I see my grandmother next to him.
50 I see my uncles, my aunts, my father's cousins,
fishing for stone beside baskets of silt and dust

as the world crumbles to pieces.
Junigihtla, junigihtla, junigihtla: thundering
up the Nantahala, up Keener, from the impoundment at Fontana,
56 from the dam at Chilhowee, at Kagley, at Hensley Lake,
from below Sylva now that Dillsboro is down.
I see them leaping the dam at Ela.
The old people are laughing, white threads of fires
rising behind them, town feast, feast of love,
60 feast of stone. Soon the dancing will begin.

→ moving to afterlife...

Smallmouth Bass   *Micropterus dolomieu*

HABITAT AND RANGE: As far south as Georgia and Alabama and beyond Appalachia as well. Seeks out rocky, often swiftly flowing streams.

DESCRIPTION AND NOTES: The smallmouth is the dominant bass of mountainous Appalachia's rivers. If the largemouth bass, which prefers the easy-chair life afforded by sluggish waters, is more familiar, that's probably thanks to many TV tournament fishing shows. And it is only in comparison to the largemouth bass that *Micropterus dolomieu*'s actually quite cavernous maw could be called "small." A bass does not seize its prey but rather endeavors to get close before opening its mouth like a bucket, exerting a suction that impels the prey backward, against its will, into the gut. How does the bass get close enough to do that? The pattern of stripes radiating back from the eyes (also found on hawks, owls, tigers, and house cats) is common in nature: it's predator-face camouflage. James Alexander Henshall, in his 1881 *Book of the Black Bass* (a classic of angler literature that anticipates later encomiums to big deep-sea fish such as swordfish, marlin, and tuna by the likes of Ernest Hemingway and Zane Grey), dubs the smallmouth "inch for inch and pound for pound, the gamest fish that swims." Few who have witnessed a hooked smallmouth fling itself high out of the water, gill covers rattling and head shaking in righteous indignation, would fail to call this species "valiant."

— *Allison Adelle Hedge Coke*

Smallmouth Bass

for Wiley Prince Jr. (1918–1978)

Immaculate.

Cream under, mossy top,
more than rock, she's queen-

detective   forehead full-on nares
crush craw powder mean   stalking machine
swallows shad roach fit.

Bronze bangled scales divine,   slim
Smallie flashes club corner tail tips, dips
red-eyed pounce on prey like
popping surface of the pond,

from now on.　　From now on
double loop knot　　hula pop-
naw, spinner　　on 8–10 test
adjustable, spin-cast—

French Broad, New-

Immaculate.

Speckled Trout

Salvelinus fontinalis

HABITAT AND RANGE: The natural distribution of brook trout is a rough quadrangle from Hudson Bay and Labrador on the north to Wisconsin and New York on the south—but with a tail of sorts extending at high altitudes along the spine of the Appalachians to north Georgia and South Carolina. The exact range and classification of the southern strain of brook trout is still the subject of study and discussion.

DESCRIPTION AND NOTES: Natives of Southern Appalachia have long held that their trout, which they call "speckled trout," is distinct from a northern brook trout; generations of ichthyologists have been taught that this is not the case. Then along came DNA research. Turns out the old-timers were right. Just as the tail region of brook trout's habitat is an outlier, so are the fish that live in it. The Southern Appalachians do have a different trout—indeed, some consider it the region's most iconic animal. Some also say the speckled trout can be identified not just by genetics but by appearance. (Another common name for the fish is "google-eye trout," and it can seem to have bigger eyes than other brook trout.) The speckled trout, an important food source for early Appalachian settlers, has had its identity somewhat obscured by decades of breeding with northern strains of trout habituated to stock streams. In the late 2010s, because of its beauty and because it is one of the area's most sensitive creatures—requiring clear, cold, clean water and forest cover—the recovery of pure speckled trout is a regional conservation crusade.

— *Ron Rash*

Speckled Trout

Water-flesh gleamed like mica:
orange fins, red flankspots, a char
shy as ginseng, found only
in spring-flow gaps, the thin clear
of faraway creeks no map
could name. My cousin showed me
those hidden places. I loved
how we found them, the way we
followed no trail, just stream-sound
tangled in rhododendron,
to where slow water opened
a hole to slip a line in,

and lift as from a well bright
shadows of another world,
held in my hand, their color
already starting to fade.

FISH

VI ~ Invertebrates

HABITAT AND RANGE: Moist leaf litter and rich soils of Appalachian forests from West Virginia to Georgia and South Carolina.

DESCRIPTION AND NOTES: Anyone who has walked in the Southern Appalachians has probably run across the region's distinctive brown, black, and yellow-banded millipedes. These eyeless and stingless invertebrates are mostly benign. When picked up, they curl into a ball and eject a brownish defensive juice that smells something like almonds or perhaps even pistachio ice cream. The ecology and evolution of the Appalachian mimic millipede complex consists of two species of *Apheloria* and five species of *Brachoria*. One *Apheloria* species is the model and contains poisons—enough hydrogen cyanide to kill a pigeon-sized bird. The other six species are copycats, dressed and along for the ride. They imitate color patterns of the poisonous species and so discourage predators—a defensive advantage and classic example of what is called Müllerian mimicry.

— *Heidi Lynn Staples*

Appalachian Mimic Millipede Credocade

How some people are just too agreeable,
mum inside an inculcated minelessness—
dear goes you blanketly erased, my good-

ness, you won't compete for a seat,
nor eat animal, milk, nor egg,
glance aslant girl, just too, agreeable

yes could stand to take a rage out of the look
of the blind mimic millipede, groundling,
soft insides invertebrate spinelessness,

yet seems defended in a full metal jacket,
gangly cyanide swagger, got guts bearing arms,
dares grow you a dangerous case, my god.

Black Carpenter Ant   *Camponotus pennsylvanicus*

HABITAT AND RANGE: Eastern North America in deciduous forests.

DESCRIPTION AND NOTES: Of the numerous species of the genus *Camponotus* in the southern mountains, the most widespread is *pennsylvanicus*. Giants of the ant world, the carpenter ant worker ranges from a quarter- to a half-inch in size with a shiny black head and thorax and a dull black abdomen with whitish hairs. A winged queen (she drops her wings once mated) may be as large as an inch. The black carpenter ant lives in hollow trees and in subterranean colonies, often invading and nesting in barns and houses. Colonies usually have thousands of ants; supercolonies in the Southern Appalachians may house up to a million ants. (One *Camponotus* colony in central Japan had five billion ants!) The carpenter ant will pinch or bite with its mandibles, but it does not sting. And, contrary to local tales in the region, it does not eat wood. Rather, the carpenter ant prefers a diet of insects and plant juice and only hollows out rotting logs and decayed wood in buildings to stake out or renovate colony space.

— Molly McCully Brown

Farthest Corner

Did you know, when it begins,
a colony has just one wingless queen,
who stripped herself of the ability to fly
when she went searching for a place
to make a home? Some little, mortal
calculus tuned sharp to instinct:
I'll be earthbound if I get to stay alive.

She seldom tunnels into sound
hard wood, but waits for the place
that asks for her body, that's already gone
some distance toward dissolving:
the farthest corners of the farthest barn,
the wasted logs yielded to rain and rot,
the oak that something else has killed

long before she came for it. She has taken herself
apart like this, flightless and fit for excavation,
to aid in the undoing of whatever needs
to go back to the earth. Every other body
that she bears will emerge suited for the same
strange task of making nothing out of something,
forging a hollow, then a perfect lack.

Imagine it: Where all your dead
and leaden things once loomed,
there is an open hillside; just where
your shoulder blade stops, smooth
and hardened, there was once a wing.

Blue Crayfish

Cambarus (Jugicambarus) monongalensis

HABITAT AND RANGE: Soft clay soils on wooded hilltops, hillsides, and springs and seepage areas. The species is known from both the Cranberry Glades and Dolly Sods, two large bogs in West Virginia. Less commonly found in Virginia and Pennsylvania.

DESCRIPTION AND NOTES: Crayfish are freshwater decapod (ten-legged) crustaceans closely related to lobsters. Spiny lobsters in Australia are called "crayfish." In Southern Appalachia, crayfish may also be called "crawfish," "crawdads," or "mudbugs." "Blue crayfish" is no misnomer for this species because it is indeed an outstanding blue. Other blue crayfish exist, but this is the only pure blue species in the region. Spectacular as it is, the creature is nocturnal, and you are not likely to see it outside of its burrow during the day. Some types of crayfish live in streams or flowing water. Others, such as this one, establish colonies under mud, building what look like chimneys on the ground above their residences. If you do encounter a crayfish, note the large front claws are used in feeding and defense—and consider whether or not you want to pick up their owner.

— *Bianca Lynne Spriggs*

Praisesong for the Blue Crayfish

Praise to your cobalt armor—to the soft
juices within churning as you churn
beneath the mud, and praise to the water
as you emerge, rinsing you vibrant again.

Praise to your sensible nature,
to your homebody ways.
You are a testament to tradition—
we would know your burrow anywhere,
little potter, your chimney stacked
mudbrick by mudbrick above
a water table, no kiln required.

Praise to the nocturnal urge that summons
you out to your front porch to admire
a summer night in the company
of neighbors—nightcrawlers, June beetles,

jarflies—among the folks who know you best,
you, too, go by many names.
You'll answer to Crawdad, Mudbug,
Mountain Lobster—it all means about the same.

I once saw an image of you on a card
between the fingers of a woman
who was fluent in fortunes.
There you were, staring up into the full
face of the moon from your front-row seat
at the edge of a midnight pool.
Wild dogs surrounded you
and your mountain was far away.
See this crayfish here, she said,
That is your courage and your uncertainty.
They are the same.

Praise to your foresight,
Cambarus monongalensis, for belonging
to more than one world, for knowing
when to make yourself at home
and when to take the moonlit path.

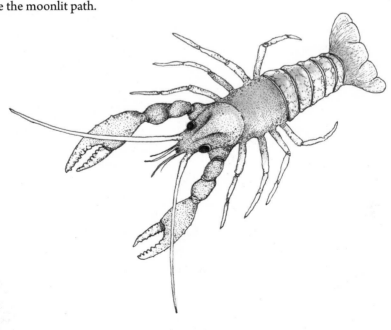

Common True Katydid   *Pterophylla camellifolia*

HABITAT AND RANGE: Deciduous forests and forested parks. From the eastern United States to southern New England, west to Texas.

DESCRIPTION AND NOTES: The katydid (a relative of the familiar grasshopper) is rarely seen because it is nocturnal and lives in trees. Its large wings resemble leaves, which help it further blend in with its habitat. Katydids mate and lay eggs in the canopy, often passing their entire lives without ever touching the ground. How most know the katydid is by his song: "kat-y-did." (Females don't usually call.) The rhythmical sound is made when the insect scrapes his forewing against a small, rigid, toothed area at the base of the wing. To some this sound is soothing; to others it is irritating. In any case, the sound can so dominate summer nights that when, just after midnight, katydids' music often stops, campers and forest dwellers wake to the eeriness of sudden silence.

—— *Kathryn Stripling Byer*

To *Pterophylla camellifolia* at the Winter Solstice

In the silence of solstice dark, while smoke
from forest fires kindled by long drought and arsonists
still shrouds our valley, you bide your time inside your cradles
of poplar and hickory. On our ridge tonight you are safe
to slumber toward equinox. Your kin, burned to ash along Dick's Gap
lie dreamless on forest floors or borne who knows where
on the wind. If you dream about anything, my small nestling
neighbors, may it be green through which sunlight, unfurling

its lifeline, awakens you, calling you forth to devour
every leafbite of chlorophyll, the whole budding forest
a feast for you. *Bon appetit*, little soon-to-be troubadours!
How else emerge into the choristers' late summer rouses,
nocturnal tree-dwellers whose mouths must keep all summer long
masticating, your leaf-wings beginning to tune up come twilight,
strumming in pure anapestic desire: *Get it on!*
Get it on! Roaming the canopy, how can the females
resist your seductions, you rock stars of late summer!

Maybe come August, I'll dare the Devil himself to come down
to Cullowhee Valley and challenge you. Maybe I'll dare
every tuxedoed fiddler in New York and Paris to match your wings
strumming a mere three hundred times every second.
Now in the silence of solstice dark, I lie in bed, sleepless
with longing for your no holds barred wing-fiddling rapture,
the forest around me throbbing again with your passion.

Diana Butterfly　　　　　　　　　　　　　*Speyeria diana*

HABITAT AND RANGE: Forests and forest margins of the Southern Appalachians from West Virginia and Virginia south to South Carolina, Georgia, and Alabama, as well as in the Ozarks.

DESCRIPTION AND NOTES: The Diana, or Diana fritillary, hatches from eggs laid on the ground rather than on the leaves of its food plant where most butterflies lay their eggs. Larvae emerge in fall. In spring they begin to eat violet plants and complete their development into butterflies. Even when they rise from the soil and twigs of the forest floor on their newly formed wings, they continue to live in the deep woods. You may see the Diana on woodland roads. Or, rather, you may see the male. The female tends to stay hidden. In addition to behaving differently, the female looks different from that male. The Diana is the most noticeably sexually dimorphic butterfly in the region, meaning the sexes are easily visually distinguished. The male is dark brown to black with wings fringed with a bright orange band with black spots. The female has a blue band with black and white spots. The female eludes not just butterfly watchers but predators too. Her appearance allows her to pass herself off as another species; it is thought that she mimics toxic pipevine swallowtails. Birds won't eat what looks like a poisonous butterfly and are fooled by the nontoxic Diana.

— *Chelsea Rathburn*

Difference and the Diana

Pattern and variation is how we come
to understand the world: light and shadow,
heartbeat and rhyme, my nursing daughter naming

my breasts Side and Other Side as soon
as she was old enough to name, marking
some difference only she could see. And in

the garden she and I now tend together,
learning our way around the plants and worms,
we think at first the butterflies who come

from the nearby woods, uncoiling their tongues
to taste our flowers, sometimes lighting on our hands,
are separate species. They look that different

flitting among our violets and lantana,
some chocolate brown and edged in orange, the others
a blue-black rimmed in shimmering blue and white.

That we are wrong, that they are male and female
and the same, their delicate spots and stripes not mirrored
but echoed in the other sex, delights us.

Darwin said when it comes to butterflies,
"the male as a general rule is the most beautiful."
Ever loyal to her gender, my daughter

would disagree on principle alone,
but the female Diana *is* lovelier,
her blue hindwings bright as a jay's tail feathers.

Even folded, she's iridescent, gleaming
beside the male whose closed wings look as plain
as pennies or dead leaves. If the male's drabness

is a kind of camouflage, the female Diana
has chosen beauty to ward off danger: her marks,
I read, mimic a toxic swallowtail,

warning would-be predators away.
My bright-eyed daughter hasn't learned that beauty
can be dangerous, the pursuit of beauty too.

How lucky she is to see the bright blue tips
of the Diana's wings and think of nothing
but the hope in her own outstretched hand.

Edmund's Snaketail (Dragonfly)   *Ophiogomphus edmundo*

HABITAT AND RANGE: An Appalachian endemic found in clear streams and rivers in only seven counties from four states—Tennessee, North Carolina, Georgia, and South Carolina.

DESCRIPTION AND NOTES: Slightly larger but closely related to the Maine and Appalachian snaketails, Edmund's snaketail grows to nearly two inches in length. Its abdomen widens at the end, so, in addition to a snaketail, it's a clubtail. (A clubtail is a characteristic shared with many of the dragonflies of its family, Gomphidae.) This clunky descriptor aside, Edmund's snaketail is actually a slender insect with distinctive green coloring. This bright existence (what we might consider beautiful) is brief, however. Most of a dragonfly's life is spent underwater as a nymph; its adult life-span is usually just a few months. Edmund's snaketail is seen on the wing only in late April and May. It spends most of its adult life feeding on small insects in the forest canopy along streams and rivers, and it is approachable primarily during breeding when it perches on river rocks. In a 1983 paper on rare dragonflies, the snaketail was described as "probably extinct"; however, it was rediscovered in North Carolina in 1994 and has since been found in South Carolina on stones along the Chattooga River as well. Described in 1951 by James Needham, author of *A Handbook of Dragonflies of North America*, the first part of the species name is an homage to his grandson, Edmund.

— *Daniel Corrie*

Dragonfly
Edmund's Snaketail

> This species is currently known only from six counties. . . . It was thought
> extinct in the 1970s and 1980s.—Giff Beaton

You wing to perch in the tree's crown,
to still as jeweled yellow-green.

Your wings are panes overlooking
current's clear and tireless pouring.

Through spring into the summer's onset,
you haunt greens' spectrum of woods

leveling to foothill's chill seams
riffling over erosions of rocks.

River's shallows ripple through rocks
for you to claim, to scud patrolling

your glinting stint of territory.
Mosquitoes' plague and fate of flies,

your hunger scans through leaves.
Your globes of eyes veer out from eras

of genes' lines past your reckoning,
launching the rush of flight to the kill.

An arrow's shaft, you fly to hunt
the targets of your four wings' course.

A phallic shaft in flight, you sheer
through air to wings arcing up

from rock's island. You clinch her.
She arches her clubbed tail to you,

pair bending to one wheel of two of you.
You circle eggs shuddering from her,

not knowing a man's name names you.
Among human numbers, you don't know

the nearing of zero. Caught in sight,
your gleaming is beauty in sunlight

over waters where instincts know
streams, rocks and trees' heights.

For now, April carries your rarity's
facet of time you are. For now, you are

a jeweled valediction, a living brooch
you give to a branch, jeweling time.

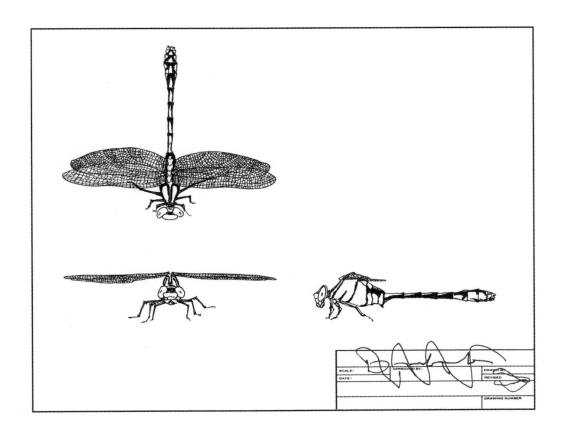

HABITAT AND RANGE: In the fine gravel or sand at the bottoms of various large rivers in eastern North America.

DESCRIPTION AND NOTES: Damming and other disturbances are over-silting the species' habitat, and pollutants from run-off in water are particularly likely to kill a mussel because it feeds by filtration, which concentrates toxins in the body. So the fat pocketbook mussel's range is declining. Where it does live, it stays in place—using a single foot that serves more as an anchor than to cover ground. Water does much of this mollusk's work. A male releases sperm into a river's current, which bears it to a downstream female. She siphons the sperm into her body to fertilize her eggs. When the eggs have grown to larvae, the female releases them to clamp onto (and feed off of) a fish. In order to attract fish, she lets a mantle—a part of her body that looks like a smaller fish, that is, prey—float outside of her shell and function as a lure. The soft-tissue creature doesn't come out of its shell much more than this. (Mussel sex used to be even more indirect; scientists have observed that many mussel species began as hermaphrodites, with the males only evolving later.) Inside its hard, protective cover and in clean water, a fat pocketbook mussel may live as long as fifty years.

— *Rose McLarney*

Fringe and Flourish

It looks like a purse, proposed the man
naming the *pocketbook mussel*.

It looks like false eyelashes, suggested another
of the soft tissue a female flaps

from her shell to be fanned by the water.
To flutter on the bottom, in the river's bed.

To say something about what strikes us,
we speak of what it is not.

This is no failing of language.
Figurative language was the first language.

Without the want to get at more
than objects a hand can gesture towards and grasp,

words would not have been shaped by mouths,
moving to sculpt a missing material.

⁓

And with her sway and sashay
the mussel means to make herself mistaken,

a metaphor. The bit of her body batted
by the current looks like a little fish

to a bigger fish on the hunt for food.
It lures him, and she looses her young,

parasites that populate his flesh.
Taking his tissue and turning it into

mussels. They will masquerade
as a fish, like their mother.

Who never touches any of them again,
which, for her, can't be called wrong.

Some young are firmly held;
some are free in the water, floating wide.

⁓

Some meanings are set; the substance
of some is liquid, the phrases lyrical.

How much of mollusk will reach fish,
of animal reach man, of woman—

it is uncertain. There are distances
it is a stretch to span.

But the mussel unfurls
her fingers. She widens her eyes.

That are faux eyes, markings on a decoy.
That are decorative fringe, not fingers.

That make us see and sense and speak
with words. Our airy flourishes

set adrift amid the amazements
with a foot in the mud of this earth.

Giant Stag Beetle

Lucanus elaphus

HABITAT AND RANGE: Eastern North America in deciduous forests. Ranges north to Ontario, west to Minnesota, Iowa, and Oklahoma, south to Florida.

DESCRIPTION AND NOTES: The giant stag beetle is one of the largest beetles found in North America. Its shellacked back ranges in color from mahogany to a dark French roast. It feeds on leaking tree sap and aphid honeydew. The male, with his distinctive, antler-shaped mandibles (therefore, "stag"), can be up to three inches in length. During mating, the giant mandibles are used to spar with and toss competing males away from a chosen female, not to kill rivals, as was previously thought. This uncommon beetle is found in mature deciduous woods and floodplain forests where rotting logs and downed trees are plentiful for breeding grounds and housing larvae. In the Southern Appalachians, the enormous pincher-jawed creature is usually seen at lower elevations, though, the truth is, the chances of seeing a stag beetle at a 7-Eleven, where it is attracted to bright fluorescent lights, are greater than seeing one in the wild.

— *Mildred K. Barya*

Black and Maroon / Stag Beetles

Friends of deadwood and seclusion,
to know you is to go underground.

It is not known why you sing in your larval form
by rubbing parts of your body together.

Perhaps that's how you speak your presence to your own kind.
So you stridulate and give off sounds and eat ginger—

a spiced life, a long childhood
before pupating and finding a new seduction—lights.

The moment you emerge you're ready to copulate.
You've spent up to six years buried under, why waste time?

Though I have seen snakes shed their skin,
never your kind discarding outer covers.

You remain a mystery even as you bare yourself to the light.
As soon as you enter new life among the woodlands, you're gone.

Luna Moth

Actias luna

HABITAT AND RANGE: Deciduous forests are the luna moth's natural habitat, but it also comes to lights in cities and towns, where it may be encountered beating against windows. Found in North America, north to Saskatchewan, east to Nova Scotia, south to Florida and Mexico.

DESCRIPTION AND NOTES: The pale green wings of the luna moth, one of the largest moths in North America, span nearly five inches. The dramatic looks of the moth are further enhanced by eyespots and featherlike antennae, though these features' purposes are functional. Eyespots confuse predators. The male's antennae, which are longer and wider than the female's, are used to detect female sexual pheromones. Only on occasion is a luna moth seen in full light; it is primarily nocturnal. When sighted during the day, it will likely have alighted on a tree trunk to dry its wings after its recent hatch from a cocoon. These wings will be used for just a week or so—the extent of a luna moth's life-span in its final form. The moth does not eat; its only purpose is to mate. However, its earlier form, a colorful caterpillar, eats the leaves of numerous trees common in the Southern Appalachians.

— *Lee Ann Brown*

Luna Moth I Am Singing to You Now

Velvety soft leafish wings
    loaded by translucent
eyespots and anthers green
    you visit only at night
a double-trunked elephant face
with outer margins pink
in southern spring brood

Caterpillar hosts: whitebirch,
persimmon, sweetgum, hickory,
walnut, sumac

Adults do not feed, only
Fly & mate & die
All in 1 short week
(no moth mouth)

Named *Actias luna* by Linnaeus
Family of Saturniidae
    (Eterniday you are related to the Silk)

Pupa means doll
& then you unfurl
to Caterpillar Alice
who rares up sphinxlike
& when threatened spits
unpleasant liquid

Alien antherish antennae
    Venusian
    You are attracted to the
Moon
A Mothra in your splendor grown
    Star Twins singing
praise songs to you
    the Unfolded field of
    your meteoric wings
once a common sight

Now I am lucky to even see you
    American Moon Moth

Thorell's Lampshade Spider   *Hypochilus thorelli*

HABITAT AND RANGE: Humid gorges with rocky cliffs.

DESCRIPTION AND NOTES: Thorell's lampshade spider is a primitive spider found in humid gorges on rocky cliffs and under overhangs. It builds a widening cylindrical web with the top rim tangent to the rock above, a lampshade-esque structure that serves as both hunting blind and fortress. The spider resides in the top of the web, hanging upside down by its two-to-four-inch legs (long and spindly for climbing in and out of the web without destroying it), which splay out from its less-than-one-inch body and monitor the web for disturbances. The toxicity of *Hypochilus* venom is unknown, but the spiders stab prey with their fangs instead of wrapping them in silk. And lampshade hatchlings trek to find their own patch of overhang or rock rather than parachuting off like the young of many spider species.

— *Gary Hawkins*

The Moonshiner, the Lampshade Spider

Well, any number of eyes on me: the bullfrog, the wood rat, the stag beetle, the wild turkeys scouring soil horizons in a line. Could be any cove in the county—its low-boiling creek and windfall acorns, where the squirrels perform their forgetfulness under a chine and wax rhododendron hell. Eyes of the hellbender, the brook lamprey, the timber rattler. The revenuer. Glance of copper, a blown husk of the still blisters through a duff of russet leaves, and shards of Mason jars silently rack tulip light winging down from the poplars. What more can they take from me? Feinting to a slant-late sun that prisons the woods, I'll nest here in its crossbars of shadows. High on the hillside, we parlor the rock with hackled webs hung out like lanterns along a porch, like the compound eyes of a homestead glinting welcome in the distance. When disturbed, a spider drops out of its protected web, crumples to the ground, feigning death. Too easy. Better to unfold from the litterfall, eyes straight ahead, reaching for no one. Time to candle up that furnace again.

VII ～ Fungi

American Caesar's Mushroom

Amanita jacksonii

HABITAT AND RANGE: Woods and woodland margins in eastern North America from Quebec south to Mexico.

DESCRIPTION AND NOTES: American Caesar's mushroom sports a shiny and smooth reddish-orange cap, gills that are pale yellow and unattached, and a fleshy ring midway around its stem. When *Amanita jacksonii* fruits, it pushes through a large white sac called the "universal veil," the remnants of which remain as the volva cupping the stem's base. It is often found growing in rings or arcs under pine and oak, midsummer through October. The Canadian mycologist René Pomerleau separated American Caesar's mushroom taxonomically from the European Caesar's mushroom in 1984. Both are considered edible species in the otherwise poisonous genus *Amanita*, but identification is tricky and amateur collectors are strongly discouraged from trying out these mushrooms in recipes. While all *Amanita* mushrooms are reportedly rich or nutty-tasting (those who survive after eating the "destroying angel" or "death cap" often say it is most delicious), symptoms of consuming *Amanita* other than a European or an American Caesar's mushroom include vomiting, dehydration, hallucinations, convulsions, organ failure, and, in many cases, death. So if you're interested in eating an *Amanita jacksonii*, best leave identification to an expert.

⟋ *Lucien Darjeun Meadows*

American Caesar's Mushroom

Amanita, Appalachia
Somewhere under pine and oak.
The universal veil dissolved.

Not fly agaric, not destroying
Angel or death cap, *Amanita*
But not maleficent,

Appalachian but not simply
American, Caesar's but not
Ruled by anyone but root

And tree and sky. Always
The red cap watching out
From this red dirt. Always

The threat of poison, the veil
Burst through and discarded,
Hollowing in upon itself

As the slender stem rises, red
And relentless as mountain sunrise,
As coal fires burning around us.

American Caterpillar Fungi   *Cordyceps sp.*

HABITAT AND RANGE: Deciduous and pine-mixed forests. Only occasionally encountered yet widely scattered through Southern Appalachia.

DESCRIPTION AND NOTES: There are as many as fifty species of caterpillar fungi in eastern North America. Knowledge of any one Southern Appalachian species is scarce, thus the information here refers to the genus in the region, not any one species. The aboveground fruiting body of the Appalachian *Cordyceps* is also called "club fungus" and "tongue fungus" because it looks like a narrow orange tongue running along the forest floor. But what feeds the species is below ground: mycelia that have encircled a subterranean moth larva or pupa and have parasitized the caterpillar, draining its essential nutrients. So, where you see American caterpillar fungus above ground, you can know an invertebrate it has killed or is gradually killing lies beneath. Related species in the Southern Appalachians parasitize beetle larvae and subterranean fungi. The Chinese caterpillar fungus, found in the high elevations of western China and Tibet, is collected every spring by the thousands because it is thought to be a heal-all and aphrodisiac. And it has become such a status symbol that dealers now sell the American species on the internet. The seemingly low-profile (maybe even distasteful-sounding) fungus is worth more than its weight in gold on the international market. These fungi are thought to be rare in Southern Appalachia but may be simply overlooked in the species-rich environment.

— *Susan O'Dell Underwood*

God as American Caterpillar Fungus

Dumb and blind, you resurrect into sunlight
out of the face of the host. Your rooted emanation
worm-shaped as the humble one you sprang from.
Isn't mimicry akin to love? Even a parasite deserves
glory, crawling your grubby scrawl of breathless
urge from dung-wet clay to elongation. Out of the big
darkness, your ochre tongue licks toward dappled shadow.
In some places the poor will rout you out, make tea
from your body, transmogrifying fungal musk and tang

into virility. Men will believe the strength in partaking
of your protrusion, erect and vivid. Commune
with the ground upon which we all kneel.
Search for the nubbin born from the wheeled spore,
life wicking up from death's mute and mutable door.

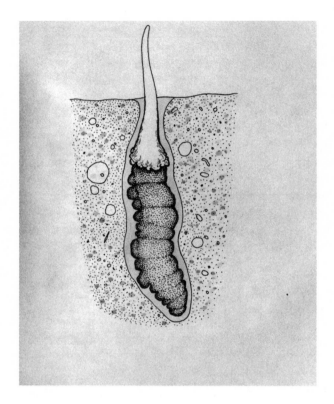

Bibliography

Campbell, John C. *The Southern Highlander and His Homeland*. New York: Russell Sage Foundation, 1921.

Catesby, Mark. *Natural History of Carolina, Florida and the Bahama Islands*. London, 1731–1743. http://cdn.lib.unc.edu/dc/catesby/.

Cavender, Anthony. *Folk Medicine in Southern Appalachia*. Chapel Hill: University of North Carolina Press, 2003.

Cooper, Robert J. "Range Expansion of the Whip-poor-will in Georgia." *The Oriole: A Quarterly Journal of Georgia Ornithology* 47, nos. 1–2 (March–June 1982).

Davis, Donald Edward. *Where There Are Mountains: An Environmental History of the Southern Appalachians*. Athens: University of Georgia Press, 2000.

Gaddy, L. L. *Alpine South: Plants and Plant Communities of the High Elevations of the Southern Appalachians*. Columbia, S.C.: Terra Incognita Books, 2014.

Gaddy, L. L. *A Naturalist's Guide to the Southern Blue Ridge Front*. Columbia: University of South Carolina Press, 2000.

Henshall, James Alexander. *Book of the Black Bass*. Cincinnati: Robert Clark, 1881.

Irmscher, Christoph. *The Poetics of Natural History*. New Brunswick, N.J.: Rutgers University Press, 1999.

Keeney, Elizabeth B. *The Botanizers: Amateur Scientists in the Nineteenth Century*. Chapel Hill: University of North Carolina Press, 2000.

Voigt, Ellen Bryant. *Messenger*. New York: Norton, 2007.

Contributors

Poets

DEBRA ALLBERY lives near Asheville, North Carolina, where she directs the MFA Program for Writers at Warren Wilson College, a program she has served as faculty member for more than twenty years. She is the author most recently of *Fimbul-Winter* (2011), which won the Grub Street National Poetry Award, and has received two fellowships from the National Endowment for the Arts, the Agnes Lynch Starrett Poetry Prize from the University of Pittsburgh Press, and a Discovery/*The Nation* prize, among other awards. A native midwesterner, she considers the Blue Ridge her true home.

MILDRED K. BARYA enjoys hiking the Appalachian trails along the Blue Ridge Parkway. When she's not in the mountains, she's at the University of North Carolina, Asheville, teaching creative writing and literature. Her publications include three poetry collections: *Give Me Room to Move My Feet* (2009), *The Price of Memory after the Tsunami* (2006), and *Men Love Chocolates but They Don't Say* (2002). Her short stories and poems have been published in anthologies, journals, and magazines such as *Tin House, Prairie Schooner, Poetry Quarterly, Per Contra*, and *Northeast Review*. She holds a PhD in English from the University of Denver and blogs at mildredbarya.com.

WENDELL BERRY is the author of more than forty books of poetry, essays, and novels. Among his honors and awards are fellowships from the Guggenheim and Rockefeller Foundations, a Lannan Literary Award, and a grant from the National Endowment for the Arts. In 2016 Berry was awarded the Ivan Sandrof Lifetime Achievement Award by the National Book Critics Circle. Since 1964 Berry has worked his family farm in Kentucky with a sense of ecological kinship and responsibility, using horses as much as possible, producing much of his own food, and writing by hand during the day to reduce reliance on electricity derived from strip-mined coal.

ADRIAN BLEVINS's third book of poems, *Appalachians Run Amok* (2018), won the Two Sylvias Press Wilder Series Poetry Book Prize. Blevins is also the author of *Live from the Homesick Jamboree* and *The Brass Girl Brouhaha*, two chapbooks, and *Walk till the Dogs Get Mean*, a coedited collection of essays by contemporary Appalachian poets and writers. She is the recipient of many awards and honors, including a Kate Tufts Discovery Award and a Rona Jaffe Foundation Writers' Award. She was born in Abingdon, Virginia, in 1964 and teaches at Colby College in Waterville, Maine.

LEE ANN BROWN was born in Saitama Prefecture on the outskirts of Tokyo at Johnson Air Base. She grew up in Charlotte, North Carolina, spent a couple of years in Heilbronn, Germany, and attended Brown, earning her BA and MFA from the university. She is the founding editor of Tender Buttons Press and the author of *Polyverse* (1999) and *The Sleep That Changed Everything* (2003). She received the Fence Modern Poets Series Prize for her book *In the Laurels, Caught* (2013), the first of a multibook project called N.C. Ode. More recent books include *Crowns of Charlotte* (2013) and *Other Archer* (2015).

She divides her time between Marshall, North Carolina, and New York City, where she teaches at Saint John's University in Queens.

MOLLY MCCULLY BROWN is the author of *The Virginia State Colony for Epileptics and Feebleminded* (2017), which won the 2016 Lexi Rudnitsky First Book Prize. Raised in rural Virginia in the foothills of the Blue Ridge Mountains, she's been writing about Appalachia for as long as she can remember. She was a 2018 United States Artists Fellow and the recipient of the 2018–2019 Amy Lowell Poetry Traveling Scholarship. An essay collection and a collaborative collection of poems with the writer Susannah Nevison are both forthcoming in 2020.

NICKOLE BROWN is the author of *Sister*, first published in 2007 with a new edition in 2018. Her second book, *Fanny Says*, won the Weatherford Award for Appalachian Poetry in 2015, and an audiobook edition became available in 2017. She is the editor for the Marie Alexander Poetry Series and teaches at the Sewanee School of Letters MFA Program, the Great Smokies Writing Program at the University of North Carolina, Asheville, and the Hindman Settlement School. She lives with her wife, poet Jessica Jacobs, in Asheville, North Carolina, where she volunteers at four different animal sanctuaries. Currently, she's at work on a bestiary of sorts about these animals, but it won't consist of the kind of pastorals that always made her (and most of the working-class folks she knows) feel shut out of nature and the writing about it—these poems speak in a queer, Southern-trash-talking kind of way about nature beautiful but damaged and dangerous.

KATHRYN STRIPLING BYER (1994–2018) lived for years within listening distance of the Tuckasegee River in western North Carolina. She began many of the poems in her first collection, *The Girl in the Midst of the Harvest*, while sitting alongside its banks. Hoot owls and whip-poor-wills sang their way into *Wildwood Flower*, her second. As she worked on her seventh collection, *Tlanuwa*, the mythic hawk of the Cherokees, rode the thermals above Buzzards Roost, the ridge on which she lived, listening at night fall to katydids chanting in the woods around her.

CATHERINE CARTER's collections of poetry include *The Swamp Monster at Home* (2012), *The Memory of Gills* (2006), and *Marks of the Witch* (2014). Her work has also appeared in *Best American Poetry 2009*, *Orion*, *Poetry*, and *Ploughshares*, among other publications. She lives in Cullowhee, North Carolina, with her husband and teaches in the English Education Program at Western Carolina University.

DANIEL CORRIE grew up spending summers in southern Virginia, where he lived during his twenties. From his camping trips as a young man, some of his most vivid memories are of the natural beauty of Appalachia and of the bleak sight of mountains that had been ravaged by strip mining. Corrie went on to settle in rural South Georgia on his wife's inherited family farm. There they grow longleaf pines and manage the farm to be hospitable for wildlife. Corrie's books are *Words, World* and *For the Future*.

JUSTIN GARDINER, originally from Oregon, married into a Southern Appalachian family. For four years he taught at Warren Wilson College outside of Asheville, North Carolina, and he now teaches at Auburn University. He has been awarded the Larry Levis Post-

Graduate Stipend through the Warren Wilson MFA Program and the Margery Davis Boyden Wilderness Writing Residency through PEN America. His poems have appeared in journals including the *Missouri Review*, *Zone 3*, and *Blackbird*. His book of creative nonfiction, *Beneath the Shadow: Legacy and Longing in the Antarctic*, is forthcoming as part of the University of Georgia Press's Crux Narrative Nonfiction Series.

LANDON GODFREY, a poet and artist, is the author of *Second-Skin Rhinestone-Spangled Nude Soufflé Chiffon Gown* (2011) and *Inventory of Doubts*, winner of the Tupelo Press 2018 Dorset Prize. A recipient of National Endowment for the Arts and North Carolina Arts Council fellowships, Landon grew up in Washington, D.C., and lives in Black Mountain, North Carolina. A grown-over clay tennis court on her otherwise wooded land serves as a way station for black bears when they head back to the Pisgah Forest after visiting local bird feeders. Every time she sees those meandering bears, Landon feels very happy. Especially when imagining the bears playing tennis.

JESSE GRAVES is the author of three poetry collections, *Tennessee Landscape with Blighted Pine* (2011), *Basin Ghosts* (2014), and *Specter Mountain* (2018). He received the 2015 James Still Award for Writing about the Appalachian South from the Fellowship of Southern Writers and two Weatherford Awards for Poetry from Berea College and the Appalachian Studies Association. Graves was raised in Sharps Chapel, Tennessee, where his German ancestors settled in the 1780s, and currently serves as associate professor of English and poet in residence at East Tennessee State University.

CATHRYN HANKLA was born in the Appalachian Mountains of southwestern Virginia, teaches at Hollins University, and is the author of more than a dozen books, the most recent of which are poetry collections *Great Bear* and *Galaxies* and a memoir in essays, *Lost Places: On Losing and Finding Home*. While living in a renovated granary on a farm west of Lexington, Virginia, she met a most persistent ruffed grouse who has haunted her ever since.

GARY HAWKINS, originally arriving in the region from the West, believed the Swannanoa Valley to be an apparition and the receding Blue Ridge to be a painting. But now, as a resident, he recognizes the geography of moisture and light—and living in Black Mountain he revels in having one of the most enviable addresses of poetry and art. From this seat, he writes poems, writes on poetry, draws, and works in letterpress, editing and producing *Croquet*, an occasional letterpress broadside delivered as a postcard. His debut collection of poetry is *Worker* (2016).

HOLLY HAWORTH's lineage goes back eight generations of farmers, millers, shoemakers, and carpenters in the mountains of East Tennessee. Several of her great-great-great-grandfathers fought in the Civil War on both the Confederate and the Union sides. One of them, Emanuel, filed a court case against Gen. Ambrose Burnside for taking eighty bushels of corn from his field while Burnside was marching his men to Knoxville. Haworth grew up in Boyd's Creek—where her family had farmed since 1807—and spent much of her life in the Great Smoky Mountains, where she later earned a naturalist certificate at the Great Smoky Mountains Institute.

ALLISON ADELLE HEDGE COKE, holding child work permits, came of age cropping tobacco, working fields and waters, and working in factories. Incarcerated as a juvenile, fostered while her mother spent a host of years in Dix and other asylums, she was the first woman in construction in 1970s Raleigh, then worked in music and landscaping, as wait staff, cashier, clerk, computer coder, commercial fisher, and night auditor. Her family hails from Rowan, Rutherford, Buncombe, Jackson, Swain, Macon, and Cherokee Counties. She also lived and worked in Mecklenburg, Wake, Moore, Johnston, Carteret, and Guilford Counties in North Carolina and in Georgia and Tennessee. Distinguished professor at the University of California, Riverside, Hedge Coke has written seven books.

SEAN HILL was born and raised in Milledgeville, Georgia, which sits in the Piedmont. His family's roots there go back to his great-great-grandfather, who was born in 1812. Those red clay hills, the waters, the animals—their songs and cries (the cicadas' drone)—the plants—their feel and smells—were formative for Hill. In part, Hill's poetry collections, *Blood Ties & Brown Liquor* and *Dangerous Goods*, explore his connections to that place and its history. It was while attending the University of Georgia that he fell in love with hiking, the North Georgia Mountains, and Southern Appalachia.

REBECCA GAYLE HOWELL is the author of *American Purgatory* and *Render / An Apocalypse*. Among her honors are fellowships from the Fine Arts Work Center, the Carson McCullers Center, and a Pushcart Prize; her books were both shortlisted for the Weatherford Award in Appalachian Literature and *Foreword Review*'s Poetry Book of the Year. Howell lives in Knott County, Kentucky, where she serves as poetry editor for the *Oxford American* and James Still Writer in Residence at the Hindman Settlement School.

LISA KWONG is a daughter of the New River Valley, born in Radford, Virginia. She grew up in her parents' Chinese restaurant, moving up from being the baby behind the cash register to waitressing there for six years after graduating from Appalachian State University. During this time, she proclaimed herself an AppalAsian. She remembers her father would stop in the road to and from their house so he could rescue turtles from being run over. Turtles hold a special allure for Kwong because she goes slow in life, carries home on her back, and retreats inside her Cancer shell for self-reflection.

JOHN LANE is professor of English and environmental studies at Wofford College and director of the college's Goodall Environmental Studies Center. Lane is the author of a dozen books of poetry and prose. He has won numerous awards, including the Southern Environmental Law Center's 2001 Phillip D. Reed Memorial Award for Outstanding Writing on the Southern Environment. He often spends time in a cabin in the mountains near Cullowhee, North Carolina, with several resident timber rattlers.

LISA LEWIS has published five books of poetry, most recently *The Body Double* (2016), with a sixth collection titled *Taxonomy of the Missing* (2018). She teaches creative writing at Oklahoma State University and serves as poetry editor for the *Cimarron Review*. She is originally from Roanoke, Virginia, where for most of her childhood and early adolescence she was puzzled every fall when the cars with the out-of-state license tags made traffic jams everywhere: what was so special about the leaves and the Blue Ridge, anyway? Her twenty-two years on the plains have answered that question with the peculiar beauties of the flatlands, and now she can be glad to have known both.

LAURA LONG was born and raised in West Virginia. Her childhood imagination was shaped by the Appalachian Mountains, and her dreams were filtered through two majestic trees, a hemlock and a maple, that filled her bedroom windows. All her writing reflects on a sense of place, including the anthology she coedited, *Eyes Glowing at the Edge of the Woods: Fiction and Poetry from West Virginia* (2017); a novel, *Out of Peel Tree* (2014); and two poetry collections, *The Eye of Caroline Herschel* (2014) and *Imagine a Door* (2009). She teaches at the University of Lynchburg.

MAURICE MANNING's collections of poetry pursue a range of topics, from Daniel Boone's story to the tradition of pastoral poetry, but all are connected to the heritage of rural Kentucky, where he grew up. Manning now lives on a twenty-acre farm in the state and teaches at Transylvania University, as well as in Warren Wilson College's MFA Program for Writers in western North Carolina. Manning, winner of the Yale Younger Poets' Award and a Guggenheim Fellowship and a finalist for the Pulitzer Prize in poetry, has published six collections of poetry. His poems are influenced by family stories and Appalachian land and heritage.

JAMES DAVIS MAY, originally from Pittsburgh, now lives at the other end of Appalachia, having moved to the mountains of northeast Georgia in 2013 to teach at Young Harris College. His house, which is at the edge of the Chattahoochee National Forest, sits about ten miles from Brasstown Bald, the tallest mountain in Georgia. He's the author of *Unquiet Things.*

DAVIS MCCOMBS was born and raised in Kentucky. He is the author of *Lore* (2016), winner of the Agha Shahid Ali Poetry Prize; *Dismal Rock* (2007), winner of the Dorset Prize; and *Ultima Thule* (2000), selected by W. S. Merwin for the Yale Series of Younger Poets. McCombs's poetry is known for its exploration of his native Kentucky's landscape and history. He has received fellowships from the Kentucky Arts Council, the National Endowment for the Arts, and the Ruth Lilly Poetry Foundation. He directs the Program in Creative Writing and Translation at the University of Arkansas and lives in Fayetteville, Arkansas.

MICHAEL MCFEE, a native of Asheville, North Carolina, was raised south of town, where he attended Buncombe County schools, wandered in the woods surrounding Arden, and hiked and camped along the Blue Ridge Parkway. He sojourned in northern Appalachia as poet in residence at Cornell before returning south to teach in the Creative Writing Program at University of North Carolina, Chapel Hill. He is the author of sixteen books, most recently *We Were Once Here: Poems* (2017) and *Appointed Rounds: Essays* (2018). He received the James Still Award for Writing about the Appalachian South from the Fellowship of Southern Writers (2009).

KEVIN MCILVOY lives near the banks of the Swannanoa River. Though he grew up in the American bottomlands, the woods and rivers of western North Carolina are his true home. For decades he has served as faculty in the MFA Program for Writers at Warren Wilson College. His novel, *At the Gate of All Wonder* (2018), is set in a part of the North Carolina Pisgah Forest designated as "the Cradle of American Forestry." His other published works include novels, a story collection, and a book of prose poems and short fiction, *57 Octaves below Middle C.*

IRENE MCKINNEY (1939–2012) grew up on her family's farm in Belington, West Virginia. She published several collections of poetry, including *The Girl with the Stone in Her Lap* (1976); *Six O'clock Mine Report* (1989), which was chosen for the Pitt Poetry Series; and *Vivid Companion* (2004). *Unthinkable: Selected Poems, 1976–2004* was published in 2009. McKinney's work is also included in the anthology *Listen Here: Women Writing in Appalachia* (2003). Her honors included fellowships, grants, and residencies from the National Endowment for the Arts, the Bread Loaf Writers Conference, the MacDowell Colony, the West Virginia Commission on the Arts, the Utah Arts Council, and the Kentucky Foundation for Women. She was appointed poet laureate of West Virginia in 1994.

LUCIEN DARJEUN MEADOWS was born in Virginia and raised in the mountains of Monongalia County, West Virginia. With German family since the 1700s in what would become West Virginia and Cherokee family in the region for generations before and after that, Meadows's home, ancestral memories, and writing are grounded in Southern Appalachia. A Bread Loaf Environmental Writers' Conference awardee, Meadows's poems have been published in national journals such as *Narrative* and *Pleiades*, as well as in place-based journals, including *Appalachian Heritage* and *Shenandoah*. Meadows lives in northern Colorado, where he loves the mountains but misses the lightning bugs of home.

SANDRA MEEK is a recipient of the Poetry Society of America's Lucille Medwick Memorial Award, a National Endowment for the Arts fellowship, and two Georgia Author of the Year awards, and she is the author of five books of poems, including *An Ecology of Elsewhere* (2016), *Road Scatter* (2012), and *Biogeography* (2008), winner of the Dorset Prize. Meek grew up in Colorado and served as a Peace Corps volunteer in Botswana. In 1996 she moved to north Georgia, where she is Dana Professor of English, Rhetoric, and Writing at Berry College, director of the Georgia Poetry Circuit, and cofounding editor of Ninebark Press.

DEBORAH A. MIRANDA is a member of the Ohlone/Costanoan-Esselen Nation of the Greater Monterey Bay Area. In 2004 she relocated from the West Coast to southwestern Virginia for love, career, and a log cabin on sixty-eight acres of land in the saddle between the Big House and Little House Mountains. When her partner's dog brought her a live box turtle in his mouth that first week, Miranda knew she'd made the right choice. Many turtles later, she continues to teach creative writing and literature at Washington and Lee University, crafting poetry, memoir, and scholarship and cherishing the Shenandoah Valley.

THORPE MOECKEL's most recent works are the nonfiction book *Watershed Days: Adventures (a Little Thorny & Familiar) in the Home Range* and *Arcadia Road: A Trilogy.*

He is author of three prior books of poetry: *Odd Botany*, *Making a Map of the River*, and *Venison*. His numerous awards include the George Garrett Award from the Fellowship of Southern Writers, the Kenan Visiting Writership at University of North Carolina, Chapel Hill, a Nonfiction Promise Award from the Sustainable Arts Foundation, and a National Endowment of the Arts Fellowship. He has settled near the upper James River in western Virginia, where he teaches in the MFA program at Hollins University, but his heart lives in the Chattooga River.

RAJIV MOHABIR grew up in central Florida and drove through the Appalachian Mountains at least once a year with his family. He is haunted by the streams that slither along the Blue Ridge Parkway, the deer that bend their necks to drink, and the bats that exodus in the evenings. Gatlinburg, Tennessee, is dear to his heart as well, as it's the first place he saw daffodils breaking through snow. He is the author of *The Cowherd's Son* (2017), winner of the 2015 Kundiman Poetry Prize, and *The Taxidermist's Cut* (2016), winner of the Four Way Books Intro to Poetry Prize and Finalist for the Lambda Literary Award for Gay Poetry in 2017. He is an assistant professor of poetry at Auburn University and lives in the southern reaches of Appalachia.

ELIZABETH SEYDEL MORGAN is a graduate of Hollins College, received her MFA from Virginia Commonwealth University, and lives in Richmond, Virginia, when she isn't at her log cabin on Long Mountain in Amherst, Virginia. Her books of poetry include *Parties*, *The Governor of Desire*, *On Long Mountain*, and *Spans*. Morgan won the Emily Clark Balch Prize in fiction from the *Virginia Quarterly Review*, and her screenplay *Queen Esther* won the 1993 Governor's Award for Screenwriting at the Virginia Film Festival. She has been a finalist for the Library of Virginia Poetry Prize and the recipient of a grant from the National Endowment for the Humanities.

ROBERT MORGAN was born in Hendersonville, North Carolina, and grew up on the family farm in the Green River Valley of the Blue Ridge Mountains. He is the author of fourteen books of poetry and nine books of prose, which have earned him many awards and honors, including three National Endowment for the Arts grants, a Guggenheim Fellowship, and a Rockefeller Foundation Fellowship, selection for Oprah's Book of the Month, and *New York Times* best-seller status. As Kappa Alpha Professor of English at Cornell, he lives in New York State. His regional work frequently returns to Appalachia for its inspiration.

SHAUNA M. MORGAN, a poet and scholar, immigrated to the United States from a rural district in Clarendon, Jamaica. She found home in the mountains, valleys, and creeks of the American South and has lived in Georgia, Florida, and most recently Virginia, where her twin daughters were born. She teaches creative writing and literature of the African Diaspora at Howard University in Washington, D.C. Her poems were shortlisted for the 2011 Small Axe Literary Prize, won honorable mention for the 2016 Salem College International Literary Awards Rita Dove Prize, and have appeared in *ProudFlesh: New Afrikan Journal of Culture, Politics & Consciousness*, *Pluck! The Journal of Affrilachian Arts & Culture*, *Anthology of Appalachian Writers, Volume VI*, *Interviewing the Caribbean*, and elsewhere. Her collection *Fear of Dogs & Other Animals* was published in 2016.

RICARDO NAZARIO Y COLÓN is a cofounder of the Affrilachian Poets. He lives in Haywood County, North Carolina, and works as the chief diversity officer at Western Carolina University. He is the author of the chapbook *The Recital* (2011) and the full-length book *Of Jíbaros and Hillbillies* (2011). His work has been published in several anthologies and online and print journals, including the *Louisville Review, Acentos Review, Falling Star Magazine, Hard Lines: Rough South Poetry* (2016), and *Black Bone: 25 Years of the Affrilachian Poets* (2017).

MARY OLIVER (1935–2019) published her first book of poetry in 1963 at the age of twenty-eight. Over the course of her long career, she received numerous awards. Her fourth book, *American Primitive*, won the Pulitzer Prize for Poetry in 1984, and her *New and Selected Poems* won the National Book Award in 1992. She led workshops and held residencies at various colleges and universities, including Sweet Briar College in Amherst, Virginia—in the Appalachian region—where for five years Oliver was the Margaret Banister Writer in Residence.

JIM PETERSON was born in Georgia and reared and educated in western South Carolina. His poetry collections include *The Man Who Grew Silent, An Afternoon with K, The Owning Stone*, winner of the Benjamin Saltman Poetry Award, *The Bob and Weave*, and *Original Face*—and he published a novel, *Paper Crown*, in 2005. He is on the faculty of the University of Nebraska MFA Program in Creative Writing and is professor emeritus at Randolph College in Lynchburg, Virginia. Peterson has spent much of his life exploring the mountains and gorges of South and North Carolina, Georgia, Tennessee, and Virginia.

ANNA LENA PHILLIPS BELL was raised in upstate South Carolina, one county over from what's considered Appalachia, on land that is mostly secondary forest. She was lucky to run around in those woods as a kid and is glad to be able to still. Her book *Ornament* is, in part, a tribute to the southern Piedmont. With her current project, *BELEAVE*, she is exploring the effects of introduced species on North American forest communities. The editor of *Ecotone*, she lives with her family near the Cape Fear River and calls Appalachian square dances in North Carolina and beyond.

MELISSA RANGE was born and grew up in the upper east Tennessee town of Elizabethton, a former rayon town that lies in a valley between Lynn Mountain and Holston Mountain, all in the Blue Ridge Mountain Range. She is the author of *Scriptorium* (2016), a National Poetry Series winner, and *Horse and Rider* (2010). She lives in Wisconsin and teaches English at Lawrence University.

RON RASH is an Appalachian writer. His place-based writing has attracted international attention, including recognition as a PEN/Faulkner finalist, the 2010 Frank O'Connor International Short Story Award, and two O. Henry Prizes. His publications include seven novels, five collections of poems, and six collections of stories. Rash grew up and studied in North Carolina and South Carolina. He now makes his home in the region of North Carolina where his ancestors have lived for centuries and teaches at Western Carolina University as the Parris Distinguished Professor in Appalachian Cultural Studies.

CHELSEA RATHBURN is the author of *Still Life with Mother and Knife* (2019), as well as *A Raft of Grief and The Shifting Line*. Her poems have appeared in *Poetry, New England*

Review, *Five Points*, and many other journals. Having grown up in Miami, Florida, with little exposure to mountains and woods, she was an unlikely transplant to Southern Appalachia, but she has made a home in the mountains of north Georgia, where she has directed the Creative Writing Program at Young Harris College since 2013.

JANISSE RAY fell in love with the southern mountains when she left her childhood home in the coastal plains of Georgia to attend college in Dahlonega, where she enrolled in a local flora course and began to hike and backpack. Although she lives in the flat woods, she is an activist for mountain wilderness, mountain biota, and mountain life. Ray is the author of *A House of Branches*, a volume of ecopoetry, and five books of literary nonfiction, including *Ecology of a Cracker Childhood*. She was the Louis D. Rubin Jr. Writer in Residence at Hollins University in 2018 and is at work on a novel set in the Blue Ridge.

GLENIS REDMOND is a curious southerner, an air force military brat raised across the United States and in Aviano, Italy. With this insider/outsider stance, Redmond often grapples with the South. She began writing poetry in Greenville, South Carolina, at Woodmont Junior High School but attributes Asheville, North Carolina, as the place where she earned her literary wings. Redmond often uses poetry as a tool to explore her place of origin. She creates poems with an acute awareness that her people were first tied to the land as enslaved inhabitants and then as sharecroppers. She keeps these injustices in mind as she writes.

RITA MAE REESE grew up in West Virginia and has also lived in Florida and California. She is the author of two books of poetry—*The Alphabet Conspiracy* and *The Book of Hulga*. She has won numerous awards, including a Rona Jaffe Foundation Writers' Award, a Stegner Fellowship in fiction, and a Discovery/*The Nation* award. She serves as the director of literary arts at Arts + Literature Laboratory in Madison, Wisconsin, designs lesbian poet trading cards for Headmistress Press, and is working on a novel about growing up haunted in West Virginia.

R. T. SMITH grew up in Georgia and North Carolina, where he earned a degree from Appalachian State University. He taught at Auburn University and was coeditor of the *Southern Humanities Review*. He now lives in Virginia, where he is writer in residence at Washington and Lee University and was editor of *Shenandoah* from 1995 to fall 2018. Smith has edited an anthology of Virginia poets and published several books of short stories and nine collections of poems, many of which are inspired by the natural and cultural environments of the South. He has received awards from the National Endowment for the Arts, Virginia Commission for the Arts, and *Ploughshares*, as well as a Pushcart Prize.

BIANCA LYNNE SPRIGGS is an Affrilachian poet and award-winning multidisciplinary artist. She is the author of four collections of poems, most recently *Call Her by Her Name* (2016) and *The Galaxy Is a Dance Floor* (2016). Spriggs is the coeditor of three anthologies, most recently *Black Bone: 25 Years of the Affrilachian Poets* (2018). She is an assistant professor of English at Ohio University. You can learn more about her work here at biancaspriggs.com.

HEIDI LYNN STAPLES spun her formative years meandering as the buzzing flitting boulders chirruping and blueberry burning bush that is the Cumberland Plateau. She lives in the Appalachian foothills of Birmingham, Alabama, on Ruffner Mountain, one of the largest privately held wildlife preserves in the United States, with her neighbors millipede, fox, owl, and imperiled tricolored bat.

DAN STRYK, originally from the Midwestern farmlands west of Chicago, now lives among the Blue Ridge Mountains in southwest Virginia with his wife, visual artist Suzanne Stryk. He has published seven collections of poems and prose parables, most recently *Dimming Radiance*. His other publications include poems in many journals and an experimental chapbook, *Field Notes*, a collaboration of poems set with corresponding images by Suzanne, and he has been included in anthologies such as *Writing on Water, Common Wealth: Contemporary Poets of Virginia, Southern Poetry Anthology: Contemporary Appalachia, CrossRoads: A Southern Culture Annual*, and *City of the Big Shoulders: An Anthology of Chicago Poetry*.

SUSAN O'DELL UNDERWOOD was raised by farmers and educators in upper east Tennessee and western North Carolina. Her grandfather was a botanist at East Tennessee University. She directs the creative writing program at Carson-Newman University. She and her husband began Sapling Grove Press, devoted to underserved writers and artists in Appalachia. She has published a poetry collection, *The Book of Awe* (2018), two chapbooks (*From* and *Love & Other Hungers*), and her work has appeared in a variety of journals and anthologies, including *Oxford American, Crab Orchard*, and *The Southern Poetry Anthology: Tennessee*.

DOUGLAS VAN GUNDY teaches in both the BA and MFA writing programs at West Virginia Wesleyan College. His poems, essays, and reviews have appeared in many journals, including the *Oxford American, Ecotone, Appalachian Heritage, Still*, and *Poetry Salzburg Review*. His first collection of poems, *A Life above Water*, was published in 2007. He is coeditor of the anthology *Eyes Glowing at the Edge of the Woods: Contemporary Writing from West Virginia*.

ELLEN BRYANT VOIGT grew up in Chatham, Virginia. She developed the country's first low-residency MFA in creative writing in 1976 and has taught in and served as the guiding spirit of that program since it migrated from Goddard College to Warren Wilson College in Asheville, North Carolina, in 1981. Among her six collections of poetry, *Shadow of Heaven* (2002) was a finalist for the National Book Award, and *Kyrie* (1995) was a finalist for the National Book Critics Circle Award. Her collection *Messenger* (2008) was a finalist for the Pulitzer Prize. She served as the poet laureate of Vermont for four years and in 2003 was elected a chancellor of the Academy of American Poets. In 2015 Voigt was awarded a MacArthur Fellowship.

GYORGYI VOROS moved to southwest Virginia after living in New York City for many years and will never live someplace without mountains again. She is the author of *Notations of the Wild: Ecology in the Poetry of Wallace Stevens* (2007) and a poetry collection, *Unwavering* (2017). She lives in Roanoke, Virginia—one of the only two cities on the Blue Ridge Parkway—and teaches at Virginia Tech.

LESLEY WHEELER has lived in the Shenandoah Valley since 1994, for most of that time in a hundred-year-old wood frame house in Lexington, with a view of House

Mountain crisscrossed by power lines. Much of her poetry engages the idea of place: real and imaginative landscapes in *Radioland* (2015); her mother's home city of wartime Liverpool in *Heterotopia* (2010); and, more recently, the racial history of her region in Virginia. Since her 2011 Fulbright in New Zealand, Wheeler has blogged about poetry at lesleywheeler.org. She teaches at Washington and Lee University.

L. LAMAR WILSON was raised on a farm in the Florida panhandle town of Marianna, where the sound of whip-poor-wills enchanted him. He's the author of *Sacrilegion* (2013) and coauthor of *Prime: Poetry and Conversation* (2014), with Darrel Alejandro Holnes, Saeed Jones, Rickey Laurentiis, and Phillip B. Williams. Wilson, a Callaloo and Cave Canem graduate fellow and Affrilachian poet, teaches on the creative writing faculty at the University of Alabama. The book he's completing animates the flora, fauna, and human kindness that defined his youth.

WILLIAM WRIGHT was born and raised in the foothills of South Carolina. Throughout his life, Wright has visited North Carolina and Tennessee's mountains so often that he has been dubbed a "Halfalachian." Wright's grandfather lived in Troutman, North Carolina, and often took Wright northwest to the highlands, where many of Wright's ancestors had lived centuries before. Wright's fascination with Southern Appalachia has only strengthened, amplified specifically by his love of the ecosystem's native flora. With Jesse Graves, Wright has collaborated on a book of poems, *Specter Mountain* (2018) and on the third volume of *The Southern Poetry Anthology: Contemporary Appalachia* (2010), which features one of the largest, most diverse collections of Appalachian poets writing today.

Artists

ALLYSON COMSTOCK's artwork is rooted in explorations of the natural world, both close to home and far away. Her Close Observation series developed while she rafted more than a dozen rivers, including a large number in the Appalachian region, and a six-week stay in Antarctica inspired the Micro, Macro and In-Between drawing series, along with a collaborative installation titled *Responding to Antarctic*. Comstock's work has been supported by a National Science Foundation Antarctic Artists and Writers Grant, fellowships from the Women's Studio Workshop, and residencies at Ucross Foundation and the Hambidge Center. Her work has been exhibited at the Czong Institute for Contemporary Art in South Korea, the Ohio Craft Museum, the Delaware Contemporary Art Center, the Mobile Museum of Art, and the Huntsville Museum of Art.

LANDON GODFREY AND GARY HAWKINS, multidisciplinary poets and artists, contributed to both the literary and visual elements of this book.

DAN POWELL's first introductions to the Appalachians were family vacations to the Smoky Mountains, which began his lifelong passion for observing nature. His light-infused landscapes owe their origin to time spent in contemplation of the natural world. Whether camping in the Shenandoah National Park, fly fishing in north Georgia streams, or drawing, he desires to lose himself in the flora and fauna. Powell's work has been exhibited in venues from Rhode Island to South Carolina. He has taught at many institutions; currently he teaches art at Georgia State University, Perimeter College.

BILLY RENKL grew up in Alabama. He attended Auburn University and the University of South Carolina, where he received an MFA in drawing. He teaches illustration at Austin Peay State University in Clarksville, Tennessee. He has traveled broadly but never lived outside of the South. Billy's work has been featured in many solo and group exhibitions, including solo shows at Cumberland Gallery in Nashville, Taylor Bercier Fine Art in New Orleans, the University of Alabama, the Jule Collins Smith Museum of Fine Art at Auburn University, and the University of Kentucky.

HENRY SHEARON graduated in spring 2017 from Warren Wilson College, outside of Asheville, North Carolina, with a concentration in printmaking. He now lives and creates art on a family farm outside of Raleigh. He enjoys all mediums but primarily works with pen and ink, creating detailed black and white drawings. He draws inspiration from everything around him, but nature, architecture, and his own dreams have always been prominent influences. He is currently experimenting with the medium of collage, recycling old drawings and turning them into new works of art.

SUZANNE STRYK has made her home in southwest Virginia for thirty years, all the while documenting her observations of the Appalachian region in her artwork. She has shown her conceptual nature paintings in solo exhibits throughout the United States, including the Morris Museum of Art in Georgia, the United States Botanic Garden in Washington, D.C., the Eleanor B. Wilson Museum in Virginia, and Gallery 180: The Illinois Institute of Art in Chicago. In 2005 a midcareer survey of her work, *Second Nature: The Art of Suzanne Stryk*, was organized by the William King Museum in Virginia.

Editors

L. L. GADDY is a naturalist based in South Carolina. He holds a PhD in biogeography from the University of Georgia (1985). He specializes in the flora of the southeastern United States but has also done fieldwork in the West Indies, Guatemala, China, and Vietnam. He is author of *The Natural History of Congaree Swamp* (with John E. Cely), *Spiders of the Carolinas*, and *Alpine South: Plants and Plant Communities of the High Elevations of the Southern Appalachians*. His books can be seen at www.tibooks.org.

ROSE MCLARNEY'S collections of poems are *Forage* (2019), *Its Day Being Gone* (2014), and *The Always Broken Plates of Mountains* (2012). Her books, inspired by the mountains of western North Carolina where she is from, have received both regional and national recognition. *Its Day Being Gone* was named winner of the National Poetry Series, and McLarney has been awarded fellowships from the MacDowell Colony, Bread Loaf, and Dartmouth College, as well as the Thomas and Lillie D. Chaffin Award for Appalachian Writing and the Fellowship of Southern Writers' New Writing Award for Poetry. McLarney is associate professor of creative writing at Auburn University and editor in chief of the *Southern Humanities Review*. As an editor, she works to offer a fresh sense of what Southern writing may be by publishing diverse selections, and as a relatively new resident of Alabama, she is learning about another area of Southern Appalachia (with more species of fish and crayfish than any other state). Rose earned her MFA at Warren Wilson College and learned about ecology growing up with a biologist father and on the banks of the Little Tennessee River.

LAURA-GRAY STREET is the author of *Pigment and Fume* and *Shift Work* and coeditor with Ann Fisher-Wirth of *The Ecopoetry Anthology*, a groundbreaking collection of historical and contemporary ecopoetics and poetry. Street has been the recipient of poetry prizes from the *Greensboro Review*, the Dana Awards, the Southern Women Writers Conference, *Isotope: A Journal of Literary Science and Nature Writing,* and *Terrain. org: A Journal of the Built and Natural Environments.* Her work has been published in the *Colorado Review, Poet Lore, ISLE, Blackbird,* and elsewhere and supported by fellowships from the Virginia Commission for the Arts, the Virginia Center for the Creative Arts, the Artist House at Saint Mary's College in Maryland, and, most recently, the Hambidge Center for the Arts and Sciences with the Garland Distinguished Fellowship. She holds an MA from the University of Virginia and an MFA from the Warren Wilson MFA Program for Writers. She is an associate professor of English and directs the undergraduate Creative Writing and Visiting Writers Series Program at Randolph College (founded in 1891 as Randolph-Macon Woman's College) in Lynchburg, Virginia, where she has lived since 1986 and loves not least because she can, in a thirty-or-so-minute drive, be hiking the Appalachian Trail or paddling the James River Gorge.

Credits

Gary Hawkins: "American Persimmon," "Black Walnut," "Ironweed," "Oconee Bells," "Persistent Trillium," "Eastern Whip-Poor-Will," "Eastern Hellbender," "Timber Rattler," "Smallmouth Bass," "Edmund's Snaketail (Dragonfly)."

Dan Powell: "Carolina Gorge Moss," "Catawba Rhododendron," "Black-Throated Blue Warbler," "Common Raven," "Great Blue Heron," "Painted Turtle," "Black Carpenter Ant."

Billy Renkl, "American Ginseng," "Canada Hemlock," "Fraser Fir," "Tulip Poplar," "Wild Turkey," "Lake Sturgeon," "Diana Butterfly," "Fat Pocketbook Mussel," "Thorell's Lampshade Spider."

Henry Shearon, "Single-Sorus Spleenwort," "Mottled Sculpin," "Appalachian Mimic Millipede Complex," "Blue Crayfish," "American Caterpillar Fungi," American Caesar's Mushroom (p. 205).

Suzanne Stryk, "Deer Mouse," "Northern Long-Eared Bat," "Southern Flying Squirrel," "Northern Cardinal," "Wood Thrush," "Eastern Newt," "Northern Slimy Salamander," "Chucky Madtom," "Speckled Trout," "Common True Katydid," "Giant Stag Beetle," "Luna Moth."